Schmidt-Focke's
DISCUS BOOK

The discus shown above was one of the early types in the development of the Schmidt-Focke strains.

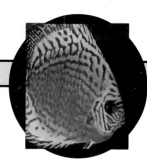

The fish on the facing page is called the 'Schmidt-Focke German red turquoise.' The body is also tall giving this fish the 'high fin' appearance.

Buckram-reinforced   Binding

·

Patent Number 4,106,148

·

Additional Patents Pending

Schmidt-Focke's
DISCUS BOOK

t.f.h. **DR. EDUARD SCHMIDT-FOCKE**

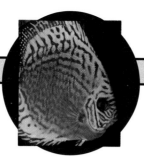

The first edition of this book was published by Bede Verlag, D-8371 Kollnburg, West-Germany. The German title was *Meine Erfahrungen mit Diskusfischen*, by Dr. Schmidt-Focke. Copyrighted in Germany in 1989.

The first English Edition was translated by Howard Hirschhorn. Additional photos were added to the English edition as well as some new text. Copyright is claimed by TFH for the translation, additional text and photographs.

TABLE OF CONTENTS

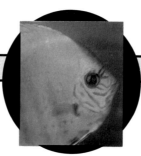

Photographs for this book have been generously supplied by Aqua Life Magazine (Japan), Prof. Dr. Herbert R. Axelrod, Dr. Martin Brittan, Dr. Clifford Chan, Bernd Degen, Oliver Deutschle, Dr. Frickhinger, Mr. Ghan, Michael Gilroy, Manfred Goebel, Lo Wing Yat, Herbert Kleykers, Hans Joachim Mayland, Theo Mee Ming, A. L. Pieter, Emerab Pischival, S.S.Rai, Dr. Heinz Reichenbach-Klinke, Fred Rosenzweig, Harald Schultz, Jack Wattley and probably a few others whom I may have forgotten... I thank everyone who helped me.
Dr. Eduard Schmidt-Focke

Preface

Dr. Schmidt-Focke is a name that has traveled around the discus world. Who among discus enthusiasts doesn't know him? His experimental crosses laid the

Left to right: Hans Joachim Mayland, Germany's foremost author-photographer of aquarium fishes. Herr Mayland has written dozens of wonderful books, including one on discus. In the center is Jack Wattley, the father of the American discus strains, especially those without stripes, called 'cobalt blues'. Dr. Schmidt-Focke is on the end.

foundation for the dissemination of this magnificent fish.

After I spoke with him for the first time in May, 1989, about his proposed

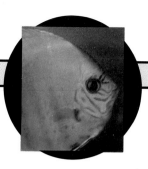

Bernd Degen is uniquely qualified to publish Dr. Schmidt-Focke's book. He is Germany's largest and most successful discus breeder and publishes books and magazines (yearbooks) on discus.

discus book, it seemed rather hopeless as I left his house in Bad Homburg. There seemed to be hardly any chance of publishing the book. Only sections of the manuscript existed, and Dr. Schmidt-Focke was undecided as to whom he should trust to publish it. He had offers from all over the world for a book that didn't fully exist.

Along with Dr. Herbert R. Axelrod of T.F.H. Publications, I visited him again the following month to discuss the project. He decided to give me the rights to his book, so work could begin on it. Splendid cooperation among us—Dr. Schmidt-Focke, his wife, Dr. Axelrod, and me—led to a completed manuscript. Schmidt-Focke's friends, who contributed photographically to this book, also deserve thanks.

This book rounds off the discus trilogy, which now consists of this book, Jack Wattley's *Neuen Diskushandbuch (New Discus Handbook)*, and my *Grossen Deutschen Diskusbuch (The Complete German Discus Book)*.

Enjoy this book, dear reader, which makes it possible for you to relive the beginnings of the discus craze.

Bernd Degen
Bede Publishers

Author's Preface

For over thirty years now, the discus—the king of the aquarium—has been fascinating me with

Symphysodon aequifasciata axelrodi, collected by Dr. Herbert R. Axelrod and Harald Schultz in the Rio Urubu, Brazil near the town of Itacoatiara, in 1958. These fish were supplied to Dr. Schmidt-Focke's brother, Hans, by Dr. Axelrod.

its majestic movement and its high stage of evolution in brood care. The numerous color variations of these fish enthralled me again and again.

In Manaus, Brazil, left to right, Willi Schwartz, Dr. Harold Sioli, G. von Lindenberg, and Prof. Dr. Herbert R. Axelrod.
Below: Harald Schultz eating the discus that died as he carried them to civilization.

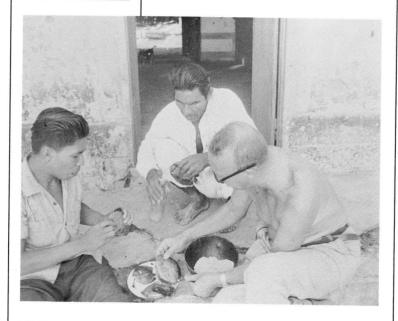

It was the mid 1950's when I succeeded in breeding the brown discus (*Symphysodon aequifasciata axelrodi* Schultz), which I reported in the aquarium magazines. Following that, aquarists from various countries visited me to discuss discus breeding.

Dr. Herbert R. Axelrod and the ethnologist Harald Schultz were among my visitors. I was a close friend of Harald Schultz until his death in January, 1966.

Harald, who lived mostly in Brazil, sent me the first *Symphysodon discus* Heckel and striped blue discus (*Symphysodon aequifasciata haraldi* Schultz). Subsequently I succeeded in breeding these unique fish.

Dr. Axelrod invited me to Chicago in 1960 to talk about my scientific work on *Betta splendens*. After that he gave me a green discus captured in the wild *(Symphysodon aequifasciata aequifasciata* Pellegrin), on whose care and breeding I reported in Axelrod's magazine *Tropical Fish Hobbyist* (Aug. 1962).

Willi Schwartz, owner of the Aquario Rio Negro in Manaus, Brazil, also visited me. Through him I received what was most likely the most colorful discus he had ever discovered in the tributaries of the Rio Purus. He called this fully striped blue discus *royal blue*.

Heiko Bleher kindly provided me in recent years with selected specimens captured in the wild, including rare color variants, such as the

discus from Rio Icana.

I owe special thanks to my old friend Professor Dr. Geisler for his help with water problems. Also, thanks to my brother Hans Rudolf, owner of the Tropicarium Frankfurt, for obtaining discus captured in the wild and making discus-rearing space and equipment available.

I've never been to South America, but I have been

Harald Schultz measuring the pH of a small pool in Brazil.

Harald Schultz with Prof. Dr. Herbert R. Axelrod.

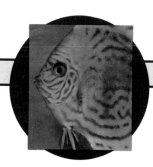

Prof. Dr. Herbert R. Axelrod with Adolfo Schwartz, the son of Willi and now the world's largest dealer in wild discus.

The author 30 years ago when he first started with discus.

Left to right, Mrs. and Mr. Hans Schmidt, brother of the author, and Mrs. and Mr. Emil Hass, in the Hass' greenhouse in Germany.

in Southeast Asia several times looking for Siamese fighting fish *(Betta splendens)* whose genetics interested me. That's why I always went by the information on discus capture sites provided by the collectors and dealers.

One could assume that after thirty years of experience with keeping and breeding discus, there wouldn't be any more problems. Unfortunately, however, that's not the case. The irresponsible

The author with a group of Indonesian fishermen on an expedition to collect wild *Betta*.

destruction of our environment places the aquarist up against almost impossible tasks. In several of the following chapters I'll describe how, with relatively simple means, discus can be kept and, I hope, continue to give us as much joy in the future.

I don't want to neglect thanking Dr. Axelrod and particularly Bernd Degen for their energetic help with the development and publication of this book. Thanks also to my wife, who read the proofs.

The author with Prof. Dr. Herbert R. Axelrod...the two great old men of the discus world.

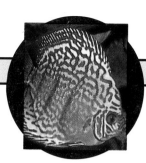

Some 30 years ago, Dr. and Mrs. Schmidt-Focke had a daughter. They named her Evelyn, after Evelyn Axelrod, at this christening.

The black betta developed by the author.

The author produced short-finned, non-pugnacious bettas (Siamese fighting fish) more than 30 years ago.

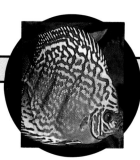

These are the kinds of discus which the author is breeding now. They have various names in different parts of the world, including the 'German red turquoise discus'.

AQUARIST PROFILES

Discus are doubtlessly incredibly fascinating fish. There's hardly an

Klaus Eckert, with a photo of his cobalt blue discus, overlaid with a light green patch under the dorsal fin.

enthusiast who can give them up. It's like a disease syndrome which is expressed in man by absolute, almost

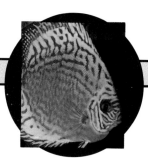

The author first gained world fame for his work with the Siamese fighting fish, *Betta splendens*. This black beauty has, unfortunately, disappeared from the aquarium scene. No one has been able to breed it since the author gave stocks to the world.

uncompromising dedication. I've got to qualify that somewhat by saying that I also met a woman among discus enthusiasts, and she was breeding them quite uninfluenced by her husband. In her honor I wrote an article in *Tropical Fish Hobbyist* magazine. Among my acquaintances, I've known of divorces due to the husband's sitting in front of the discus tank and staring into it instead of devoting himself to his family when he came home after work.

I'm also familiar with a suicide attempt when a professional discus

breeder failed after having invested everything in specimens and breeding facilities. He was saved and spent some time under psychiatric care. Another discus breeder used his swimming pool for regular water changes, but he wasn't very successful with this wasteful method. One day he set out for Thailand. Television showed his photograph . . . as a missing person. He's said to live in Spain now and owns a fine villa there.

A confused discus aquarist wrote me from Australia. He sold his car to be able to finally afford

healthy discus. The first ones he got spawned in the quarantine tank all right, but they produced no progeny. Then he wrote me that now he was going to sell his house, because the water where he was living wasn't suitable for breeding discus.

A physician, a Dr. Klaus from Dillenburg, Germany, finally succeeded, after much effort, in breeding a large number of blue discus. The full coloration of those discus was delayed. He offered them for sale to a wholesaler when they were only three months old. As the doctor stood there at the wholesaler's establishment, the buckets of discus in his hands, his world collapsed around him as the dealer refused to buy the weakly colored young discus. Since the small fish were already clearly suffering from oxygen deficiency and taking them back home was out of the question, he simply gave them to the dealer. His wife was horrified. Hesitantly, he asked the dealer for at least a few small green discus from the dealer's tank in exchange. With these fish, which attain their color early, he didn't have any luck. They grew poorly and died miserably. These fish were probably treated very early with hormones or pigments. Despite all that, this friend of mine continues to be an enthusiastic discus fancier who spends a great deal of time and

Prof. Dr. Herbert R. Axelrod with Mrs. Annaliese Schmidt-Focke, in the fish room of the author's home in Bad Homburg, Germany.

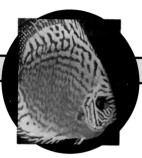

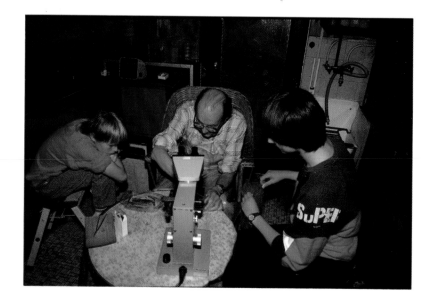

Beginners should buy and use a microscope. They will need it for the identification and cure of discus diseases, and for the proper handling of live foods.

Dr. Dieter Untergasser's book on *Discus Diseases* is considered the best book on this subject. It was originally published in Germany by Bede Verlag, the original publishers of Dr. Schmidt-Focke's book.

money on his hobby.

Fish retailers and wholesalers often inadvertently buy sick discus from aquarists. Since it's not always possible to keep discus optimally under the conditions imposed on the commercial dealer, he always has more problems with fish obtained in this way (from private parties), and he's not willing to pay higher prices. That's why dealers usually offer ridiculously low amounts of money to frustrated discus breeders who come to them. These low prices often don't even cover the expenses. Discus fanciers, on the other hand, often pay far too high a price when they buy.

I'd recommend the purchase of a microscope to all discus aquarists. Beginners can easily recognize gill and intestinal worms. The procedure is explained in the book *Discus Diseases* by Dr. Dieter Untergasser.

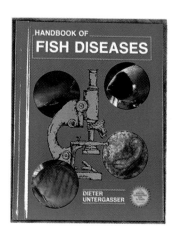

HERBERT HAERTEL, THE FIRST GERMAN DISCUS BREEDER

A "blue angelfish" was what he called his first discus, and that's why he paid a high price for it. Herbert Haertel was the owner of a tropical fish shop in Dresden before World War I. He went to New York himself to get his dream fish, which was a tiresome ocean trip then, sailing to New York and back again to Germany. The fish survived the rigors of the trip, thanks to the care they received.

They were probably brown discus. After a richly varied diet, they soon spawned. As with angelfish, which were being successfully bred at that time, Haertel removed the clutch of eggs and tried to induce hatching by means of aeration. With this method, naturally, he had to fail.

More discus were obtained by a Hamburg tropical fish breeder and turned over to experienced angelfish breeders, whose efforts likewise failed. Tap water in Dresden was hard, so Haertel obtained softer water, and in that water the first fry finally hatched. They died because they didn't eat any infusoria or *Bosmina* (one of the freshwater crustaceans generally lumped under the name water fleas). Haertel tried in vain to combat egg fungus with drugs.

He finally built a large clay pipe, which he gave the fish to spawn in. The discus spawned inside the clay pipe and came out again only when the fry were swimming free.

Now Haertel could see that the little discus were eating the slime that they nibbled off the parents' skin. For him, the riddle of discus breeding was resolved. Presumably, he succeeded in breeding them in 1933. Thirty-two young discus survived. With these aquarium-bred discus, he tried for a long time to breed further, but he didn't succeed again.

Harald Schultz, My Friend The Ethnologist

Harald Schultz, aquarist and ethnologist who studied the Brazilian Indians, was the son of a German physician who emigrated to Brazil. Harald, for me, was one of the most genial people I've ever had the good fortune of meeting. We were intimate friends until his untimely death. I admired his idea of

Harald Schultz photographed these Indians as they 'hunted' for discus. Discus are usually collected one by one.

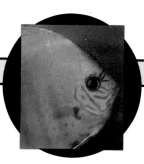

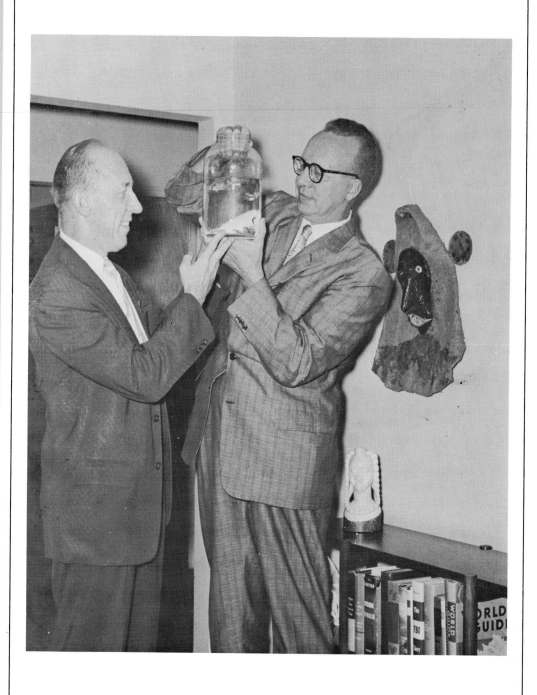

Harald Schultz, right, with Frank Alger of guppy fame. This historical photo was taken in the home of Prof. Dr. Herbert R. Axelrod in 1958.

protecting Indian culture from the disruptive effects of civilization and of communicating their cultural values to the rest of us. Harald was exceedingly talented, just like his brother, a botany professor.

Harald Schultz described, in his book *Hombu*, the life of Indians who lived at the edge of white civilization. *Hombu* means *look at us* in the language of the people he was studying. This book, with its unadulterated, informative, and wonderfully candid photographs, is really a historical document. His articles also appeared in *National Geographic* magazine. His fifty-two films are archived at the Scientific Film Institute in Gottingen.

Harald discovered the splendidly colored blue discus in the interior of the inaccessible jungles of the upper Amazon. These blue discus were named after him—*Symphosodon aequifasciata haraldi.*

He transported eighty-five of these gems in metal canisters under the most difficult of conditions through the jungle for three thousand

kilometers (1800 miles) to São Paulo. He and his Indian companions ate the discus that died along the way.

When he arrived home, the coloration of his discus was so bright that he at first thought they were in breeding color. That was a mistake. It turned out that these discus were brilliantly striped in blue. Unfortunately, all of the wild specimens that survived the long trek eventually died of the many injuries they suffered en route.

After I successfully bred brown discus in 1955 I met Harald through Dr. Herbert R. Axelrod. Harald was particularly interested in the brood care of these fish, since he was never able to observe it in the wild. Although he

Harald Schultz coaxed all of the Indians to search for discus in the wilds of Brazil.

The author's first breeding of *Symphysodon aequifasciata haraldi.*

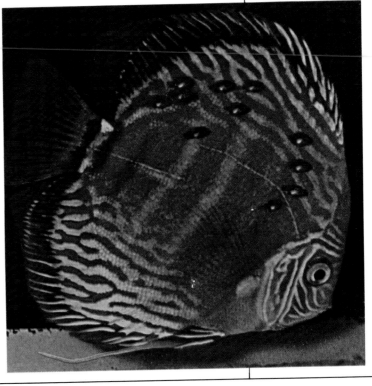

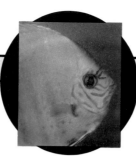

The *Symphysodon aequifasciata haraldi* which might well have been the first living fish of this species outside Brazil. It was successfully bred by the author. (Same fish facing page.)

was Brazilian, he had gone to school for a few years in Germany, and that brought him back to Germany from time to time.

He once told me, "I'll send you even more beautiful discus which I've seen in the Rio Téfé area and the upper Amazon." He described these discus in the most splendid of colors and with the fertile fantasy of a poet. Harald kept his word.

In November 1959 three practically unharmed discus arrived at the Frankfurt airport in Germany. They were magnificent fish. In another chapter, I'll describe how they were bred.

Harald not only relentlessly protected the Indians, but also our fish. During an expedition to capture fish, a hostile

The author's famous photo of the brown discus pair, *Symphysodon aequifasciata axelrodi.*

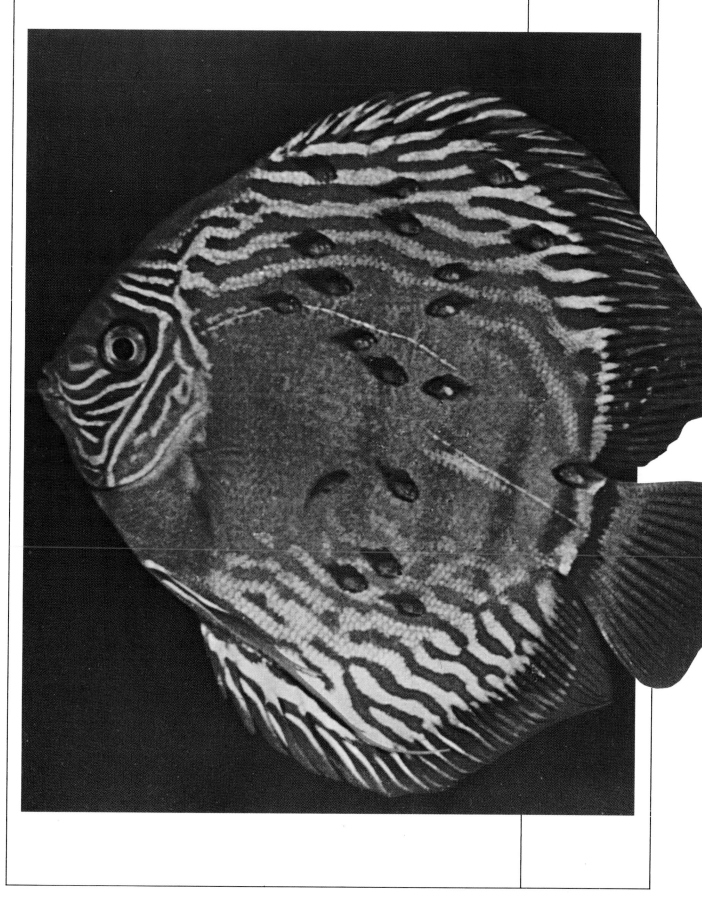

One of the brown discus, *Symphysodon aequifasciata axelrodi* bred and raised by the author. These were the first discus bred by the author. It is much easier to breed from tank-raised fish than from wild ones.

Top, facing page: The author with Jack Wattley.

Bottom, facing page: In 1958, Prof. Dr. Herbert R. Axelrod returned from Téfé and the Rio Negro with four different color varieties of discus. In those days the fish were carried in 5-gallon metal cans with holes cut in the sides.

Indian inflicted an about 50-cm wound in Harald's back. The Indian sliced open Harald's back with a machete; he once showed me the nasty-looking scar. Friendly Indians brought Harald, severely wounded, to Manaus.

One day, during the last few years preceding his death, I received a call from the airport telling me that I was supposed to pick up a severely ill passenger. It was Harald. We brought him to the University hospital. His kidneys had failed.

He was saved and recuperated rapidly. We went with him during his convalescence in Switzerland, and he was soon again the old idealist. He gave lectures to the other hotel guests on his Indians and on discus. Under the auspices of the Anthropological Museum in São Paulo, he had made expeditions to then unknown Indian groups and had had to endure unbelievable hardships.

Harald sometimes suffered from bouts of malaria, since when he had started going into the jungles there weren't any effective preventive or therapeutic antimalerial drugs available. He finally

died, much too soon, at 56 years of age. Harald had little feel for material things. It's only because of the constant support by Dr. Herbert R. Axelrod and his worldwide connections that Harald's superhuman achievements became known throughout the world. Perhaps Harald made things a little better for his friends by his exemplary devotion to his magnificent task.

Jack Wattley, U.S.A.

Jack Wattley and I made each other's acquaintance after I had, years earlier, obtained Jack's finest bred specimen, a turquoise discus, from a Honolulu dealer. I was thrilled, and we've been meeting every year to exchange experiences.

Jack was probably the first aquarist who realized how important artificial breeding is for discus when we want to prevent the transmission of diseases from parents to young. Jack also, participated in South American trips to capture wild specimens, and that's where he discovered the giant discus in the Rio Jurua, bred specimens of which he brought to me. I'm always glad when Jack visits and regales us with his amusing anecdotes.

Lo Wing Yat From Hong Kong

Lo Wing Yat is an enthusiastic discus breeder with a great deal of experience. He works along with his friend Ng to handle the demands of the business. Their motto is: Keep it as clean as a hospital.

Their cobalt blue discus, among other varieties, are the fine result of inbreeding with purposeful selection. He works with reverse osmosis, considering that the Hong Kong metropolitan water supply is no longer suitable for discus breeding.

Herbert Kleykers shown below admiring *Pterophyllum altum*. Up to now this fish has never been spawned in an aquarium. The center spread is one of Kleyker's aquariums in which he keeps the Schmidt-Focke discus.

Herbert Kleykers From The Netherlands

Herbert Kleykers is indeed one of the most congenial of aquarists, self-effacing and idealistic. In 1974 he received his first red-turquoise discus from me. His fish came out red-brown and striped with green. The accented fifth middle stripes of my crosses of *S. a. haraldi* and *S. discus* didn't show up again with him, either. Meanwhile, he bred high-fin discus from the specimens I obtained for him from Jack Wattley and Lo Wing Yat.

The Netherlands has great water problems as far as discus are concerned. Herbert Kleykers's experiences with damage caused by water, feed, and medications match my own. Herbert detoxified his tap water with activated charcoal and reverse osmosis.

Emran Pishvai, U.S. Breeder From Iran
Emran Pishvai deals especially with diseases of discus and their treatment. He visited me to select discus to take with him.

S.S. Rai From Selangor, Malaysia
S.S. Rai has bred all discus varieties. He plans to release bred progeny of captive wild specimens in order to maintain the purely natural colors.

Mr. S.S. Rai, a Malaysian aquarist who has been seriously affected by 'discus-fever.'

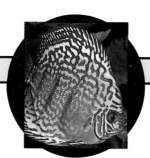

The author with Jack Wattley in front of the author's home. Wattley became famous worldwide when he produced the turquoise discus shown to the right.

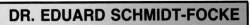

The two discus shown to the left are typical Oriental cobalt blue turquoise discus. The fish below is the cobalt blue discus darkened up because the fry are feeding from her side.

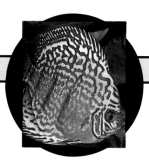

Gan Khian Tiong is one of Singapore's most successful discus breeders. He is assisted by a physician, Dr. Clifford Chan.

Dr. Clifford Chan and Gan Khian Tiong

These two well-known breeders from Singapore produce mainly solid-colored, highly bred discus. Mr. Gan owns a very large discus breeding farm.

Years ago I visited discus breeders in Thailand and Singapore. I was impressed by the size, health, and fertility of the fish I saw. There were, however, no particularly colorful discus strains, just mainly brown ones and crosses with striped discus. Food and water conditions were optimal. It was new to me to learn that 80% of the tank water there was renewed every day with tap water. That prevented disease. I also learned from Dr. Chan that experienced discus breeders are still carrying out these extensive changes of water. They use neither filters nor heaters. I learned from the experiences of Thai discus breeders just how important the constant change of water is for limiting the spread of diseases.

Gan Khian
Tiong's
magnificent cobalt
blue discus.

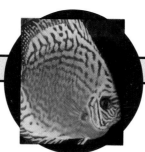

This historical moment was the first breeding of *Symphysodon aequifasciata haraldi,* the so-called blue discus. The author succeeded in breeding these wild fish. Most of the fancy blue and turquoise varieties came from these fish.

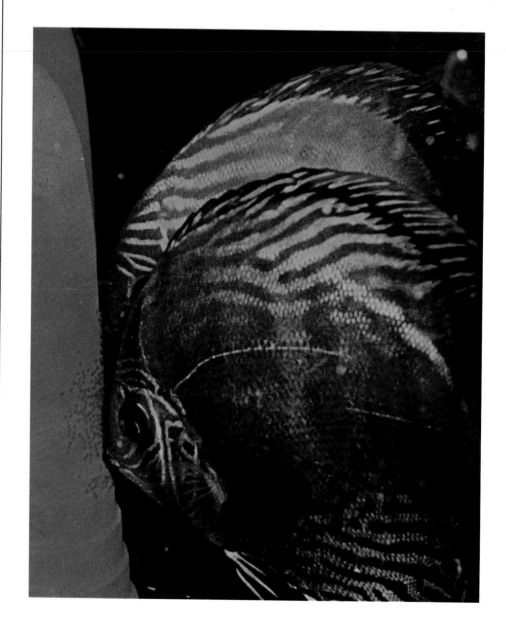

How I Began with Discus

My brother Hans Rudolf and I inherited our interest in nature from our grandfather, a teacher, who taught us

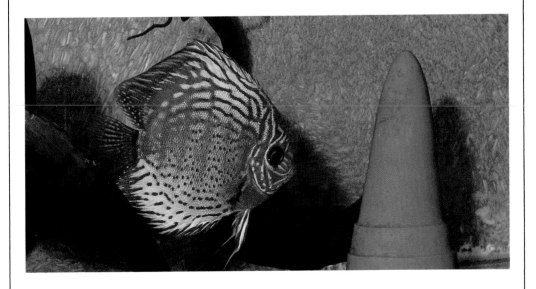

A green discus from the Rio Putomayo.

how to identify plants and to recognize birds by their calls.

I kept fish as long ago as

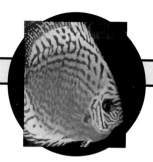

Bernd Degen, in the red shirt, with the author, Dr. Eduard Schmidt-Focke. Originally born as Eduard Schmidt, he added his wife's maiden name, Focke, to his own since his wife was the last member of her family and no one else could carry on the family name. Such is the generosity and thoughtfulness of this gentle man.

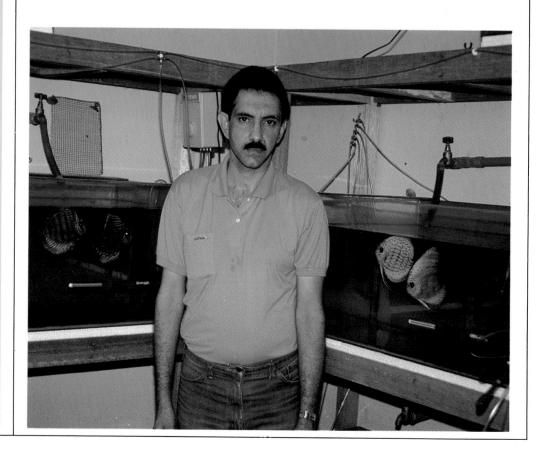

S.S. Rai from Malaysia with his gorgeous discus.

after World War I; much to the dismay of my parents, I kept them in an old bathtub. I didn't have any money then for an aquarium. Glowing coals provided heat, for there weren't any aquarium heaters available. And I suffered from carbon monoxide poisoning because of that coal heating.

During the school year, my aquarium stood in the classroom. Even during the closing exams in preparation for college, I wasn't about to relinquish giving a talk on the Mendelian laws of inheritance in Siamese fighting fish.

Though my own six children don't show any clear-cut interest, my grandson Marc has been working with tropical fishes since he was eight years old. (It's conceivable that the free combination of genes is expressed in the second generation. American investigators, unequivocally against dominance in heredity, had to admit, following controlled trials, that human traits are due 70% to genetics and only 30% to ambient factors. Observations involving identical twins who were brought up separately in different environments play a significant part in these conclusions.)

In World War II I took my valuable fighting fish and gambusias to the Caucasus with me and used them there to fight malaria. About 10% of our troops had malaria at that time. After the Russians surrounded us, I also fell ill and was flown back home with the wounded and with my valuable betta line stock.

During my training as a medical specialist, I investigated the effects of inbreeding in fighting fish and in mice that I exposed to high doses of X-rays.

At the University of Hamburg, Professor Schulz and I were looking for a suitable culture medium for the gonorrheal pathogen, *Gonococcus*. We injected the ovaries of fighting fish females with these organisms and kept the fish at a water

A crossing of *Betta splendens* with *Betta imbellis*. The offspring shown here were magnificent. The author gave up breeding *Betta* for discus breeding since his medical practice didn't give him enough time or space for both.

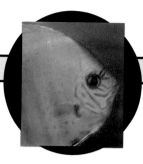

Two of the African clawed frogs on which the author experimented. The *Xenopus* is shown above while the *Hymenochirus* is shown below.

temperature of 36°C (96°F). The gonococci multiplied—showing us that we had the medium in which to culture the pathogen, a necessary step to effectively controlling gonorrhea.

A pigment-cell tumor formed in a male of the inbred betta line. As reported elsewhere, it could be transmitted only to fish of this one inbred line. Other betta lines rejected the tumor. They apparently had enough resistance. Professor Breider from the University of Wuerzburg diagnosed it as pigment-cell cancer (guanophoroma).

In order to determine the effect of hormones on tumor growth, I removed the ovaries from female bettas under anesthesia. To my surprise, these females turned into fertile males in three months' time. Mated with females, these "new" males produced only female offspring.

The histological studies were done by Professor Klatt, an assistant at the Zoological Institute in Hamburg. These studies showed that the altered betta developed a single active testis in which perfect sperm cells were demonstrated.

These concerned with animal welfare—and I include myself among them—may object to these studies. Without a minimal amount of animal studies, however, there'll not be any progress in

The author on an expedition to Indonesia to look for more varieties of *Betta*.

human medicine, either. The important thing, to me, is that the animals do not suffer, so they have to be operated on or treated under anesthesia.

By using African clawed frogs, I was able to significantly cut down the waiting time for a pregnancy test. I spoke on this subject at the Gynecological Congress following the war. Based upon the results of these studies, I was invited to work at a university clinic, but I turned down that way of continuing my work considering the hot competitive atmosphere at such clinics.

My preoccupation with fish caused my medical associates to ridicule me. At one party they tied me up and urinated in my aquarium tanks. Things were bad enough as they were because of the cleaning ladies, who often refused to enter my room. There were bottles of frogs under the bed and bird cages (with mice in them) hanging on the walls, so I couldn't blame the cleaning ladies too much.

After my training I went to Frankfurt/Main and bred fish in my brother's Tropicarium import-export firm, where I successfully bred neons, chocolate gouramis, and brown discus. Some time later I was licensed and opened a gynecology/obstetrics practice in Bad Homburg.

Harald Schultz sent me

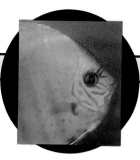

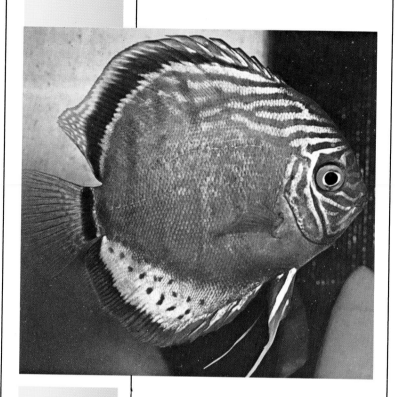

The photos on these two pages are early attempts by the author to photograph his discus. The fish above is a green discus, *Symphysodon aequifascista aequifasciata*, they come from the western end of the Rio Negro system in Lake Téfé. The fish on the facing page is *Symphysodon aequifasciata haraldi*, the blue discus.

the first blue-striped discus, and from Dr. Axelrod I received the first green discus specimens. I kept both subspecies in soft mountain water that I laboriously lugged down from the Taunus. My wife bred the green discus while I was away at a meeting. The result of hauling all the water, besides successful breeding of discus, was two hernias. The double burden of practicing medicine and of breeding fish led to a stroke years later.

In closing this chapter, I'd like to describe some of the experiences from the discus-breeding facilities at my home in Bad Homburg. To keep and breed discus, temperatures between 28 and 30° (82 and 86°F) are

essential. For years I underestimated the high rate of water evaporation at these temperatures. In one of my aquarium rooms are 18 tanks of different sizes. At first I noticed water spots on the ceiling of a few rooms. I bought an electric dehumidifier for the room, which removed about 10 liters of water daily from the air. But in vain! The attic was constantly moist. Condensed water dripped from there down into the rooms below. Only when a chimney sweep fell through the attic floor did I install an exhaust fan in the ceiling. It was supposed to draw off the moist air and lead it outside. This system is reliable. Since then, the glass sides of the tanks haven't fogged up any more. Roof repairs, as well as inside and outside wall repairs, were so expensive that even successful discus breeding didn't make enough money to cover the expense.

The author with
Lee Chin Eng in
Indonesia.

Keeping Discus

WATER PREPARATION

Before I began practicing medicine, I searched around in

The discus with the wide stripe is *Symphysodon discus discus*, the fish everybody calls 'Heckel' because Dr. Haeckel first described it. The other discus is the blue discus, *Symphysodon aequifasciata haraldi*.

Germany to find suitable water for discus, and I found it in Bad Homburg at the foot of the Taunus Mountains, a quartzite

Bernd Degen's Torfbombe (peat bomb) which rids the tank of dangerous heavy metals. The large blue can is a natural biological filter cannister.

formation. The spring water nearby had a conductivity of 40 microSiemens and a pH of 6.0. I brought this water home myself in canisters several times a week. Before that, I lived in Frankfurt, where the water conditions were much more unfavorable than in Bad Homburg. Professor Sterba built me a partial demineralizer, but I wasn't able to breed discus in partially demineralized water; I was successful only with spring water.

Professor Geisler led me to try breeding with a "peat bomb." Peat binds calcium, magnesium, and also trace metals. The best for me was unfertilized high moorland peat. After a short rinse of the peat

water, I was able to reduce the conductivity of my tap water from 150 microSiemens down to 30 microSiemens. The pH dropped from 8.0 to 6.5.

Not all peats appear to be suitable. With a peat from Russia, the conductivity rose to over 300 microSiemens. The important point is that the peat come from still unburdened deeper layers. Upper layers are already severely contaminated by rain.

That's how I bred my discus for years. In the meantime, I'm not quite certain any more about whether the quality of my tap water hasn't deteriorated because of difficult-to-demonstrate environmental toxins. The conductivity of my tap

Prof. Dr. Rolf Geisler who studied the discus and helped the author considerably in his initial studies.

water has risen to 180 microSiemens.

Today I let my tap water first run over activated charcoal. That causes the pH to rise, but it falls again after the water runs through the peat. Meanwhile I'm using water half from a reverse osmosis unit and half from peat water. I mix the two waters in a 1000-liter tank that stands in a furnace room. A garden pond pump lifts the improved water from the cellar to my aquarium tanks.

According to my nephew Bernd Schmidt, a biologist, activated charcoal removes about 50% of toxic substances from the water, about 20 to 30% is removed with peat, and about 80 to 90% is removed with reverse osmosis.

Reverse osmosis gave me water with a conductivity of 25 to 30 microSiemens and a pH of 6.5. Water prepared with reverse osmosis reduced the same proportion of all ions in the tap water.

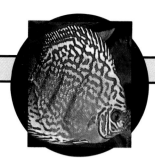

Bernd Degen on an expedition to catch wild discus in Brazil. Working on the Rio Negro, he uses a reverse osmosis machine to take Rio Negro water back to Germany for further study.

DR. EDUARD SCHMIDT-FOCKE

KEEPING DISCUS IN COMMUNITY TANKS

Regardless of what type of gravel you use, bottom cover always provides breeding grounds for parasites, so don't use it.

It's wise to populate the tank only with the progeny of one species. Community arrangements with other species of tropical fish is inadvisable, but neons can enliven the scene for the observer. They come from a similar biotope as the discus, and up to now they haven't been affected by the new "discus disease." Angelfish, though, can transmit diseases to which discus are very susceptible. Catfish, which are supposed to scavenge up food remnants, become superfluous if the bottom circulation runs properly to the inside filter; the inside filter is cleaned daily with hot water, thus destroying the pathogens that gather there.

Oak roots from a moor are suitable as decoration. These roots should stand on thin legs so that no debris builds up on them. Plants can be attached to these roots if the light is adequate. The surface of the water can be covered with water sprite (*Ceratopteris*) to soften the incidental light. Stems of *Philodendron gigantea*, placed over the tank, dip down into the water and develop into a maze of roots that cleanse the water of the decomposition products of metabolism.

Many people like to keep their discus in a community aquarium. The problem with such tanks is the gravel on the bottom. This gravel always provides breeding grounds for parasites and it is best if you don't use it.

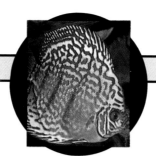

THE BREEDING AQUARIUM

A thoroughly cleaned 100-liter (about 25 gallons) tank suffices for a breeding pair. It shouldn't be lighted, but it should be protected. Two to three clay cones, which go into one corner, have worked well for deposition of eggs, according to my experience over the thirty years I've used them. Prepared water is then added. I breed at a conductivity of 50 to 70 microSiemens and a pH of 6 to 6.5. The weakly acidic pH is achieved by passing the water over high moorland peat or by dropwise addition of a natural acidifier such as phosphoric acid. Previously, I put the breeding pair into a short bath of salt or potassium permanganate to free them from at least some of their ectoparasites. Formalin (diluted formaldehyde) was more effective, but then the discus should only be treated two or three days after transfer, because netting always causes mucous membrane wounds, through which formalin could even cause death. Carry out short baths only under direct visual supervision. Recently, I put a breeding pair into a Flubenol bath for a day. Short baths won't kill intestinal parasites.

These discus are the results of crossing the *Symphysodon discus discus* with the *Symphysodon aequifasciata haraldi.* Unfortunately the undesirable black bar marking persists for several generations.

Intermediate generations of green discus, *Symphysodon aequifasciata aequifasciata*, on their way to becoming turquoise discus without stripes.

THE PEAT "BOMB"

Peat bombs are tightly closeable plastic containers used industrially to store wastes. A water exit port in the lid and a water entry port at the bottom have to be made. These "peat bombs" range in size from 30 to 100 liters (7½ to 25 gallons). The water, which has to pass first over activated charcoal, must enter the peat bomb slowly or the lid might pop. While monitoring conductivity, let only enough water flow through to reach an optimal value. Water having a high conductivity rating at the outset won't improve after only one run. In that case, peat water can be diluted with water from the partial demineralizer or the reverse osmosis unit. With water initially at 150 microSiemens I obtain a drop to 30 to 35 microSiemens.

Use only unfertilized white peat. During long periods of interrupted water flow, decomposition products form in the peat. Softening of the water and toxin absorption depend upon the amount of daily flow. Conductivity rises again once the peat is exhausted. The peat must be sealed at the top with Perlon wool, over which I lay a perforated lid.

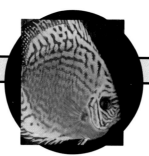

Dr. Eduard Schmidt-Focke's famous photograph which appeared in *Tropical Fish Hobbyist* magazine in 1961 (German edition), shows his first pair of *haraldi* spawning. The young are eating the slime from the parents body in this photo (part of a series).

Raising Discus

WET NURSE/FOSTER PARENT CARE

You always hear that discus eat their fry, and

Most discus can be trusted with neither their eggs nor their fry. But the great pleasure one gets from watching the interplay of the parents and their fry is immeasurable.

they are known as egg-eaters. This confusion of instinct occurs particularly often in the

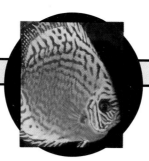

A hybrid German red turquoise with its fry about one month old.

captive young offspring of fish caught in the wild. I've received reports of up to twenty clutches, laid at weekly intervals, being eaten. Fertility, especially of the females, is high, while the males hardly even fertilize later clutches. If pairs eat two of their clutches successively, separate them. Eggs can be taken away from egg-devouring parents, too.

The situation often occurs when the young of particularly valuable discus have to be rescued. The eggs are transferred to a glass tank and well aerated. The unfertilized white eggs are picked out with the point of a sewing needle, thus preventing the clutch from becoming moldy.

When the young swim free, they can be turned over to a pair of "foster fish." These foster parents are naturally caring for their own brood at the moment. If those young

This brown discus, *Symphysodon aequifasciata axelrodi*, with her young.

are larger, they have to be removed first. Then the "orphans" can be placed in the care of these particularly good parents. It's important to balance out the pH and conductivity to avoid the fin damage which the newcomers could suffer. In this way, I was able to let these good foster discus parents save three broods from different parents.

ASIATIC METHOD OF PROTECTING EGGS

In Thailand I saw how egg-eating was controlled with wire screening. The mesh was about 5 mm. The screen was at such a distance from the clutch that the parents could see but not touch the eggs. Hatching larvae hung wriggling from the pot, stimulating the discus parents' brood behavior. In my tests, about half of the parents accepted the free-swimming young discus.

Southeast Asians are excellent tropical fish breeders with a long tradition. Their conditions, though, are much more favorable than ours. Warmer climate, adequate live foods, and, above all, soft, weakly acidic tap water make fish breeding considerably easier.

The most fascinating discus breeders I ever met were Japanese from Narita. They visited me, led by B. Tokiyama, manager of Far East Enterprises, Inc., and photographed uninterruptedly in and around my breeding facilities. They brought me gifts of a geisha doll in

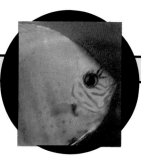

Jack Wattley, America's first and foremost discus breeder, with his latest strain, the metallic turquoise discus.

a glass box and very valuable veiled-tail goldfish, which are highly bred forms Japan has been breeding.

ARTIFICIAL RAISING OF DISCUS

In 1960 Dr. Axelrod kindly brought me to the American Henry Madson in North Chicago, the first breeder who succeeded in artificially raising discus with powdered egg. I could hardly believe what I saw. Young discus just a few days old, without their parents, were swimming around in a 100-liter tank of water. Madson had strewn powdered egg into all four corners of the tank, and it was eaten by the young discus. I don't remember whether the parents, too, were artificially raised or not. The young were conspicuously small brown discus. When I returned home, I tried artificially raising discus with German powdered egg, but I didn't succeed. The young died on the fourth day after swimming

DR. EDUARD SCHMIDT-FOCKE

In Thailand and other southeast Asian countries, it is not uncommon to see discus spawns covered with a wire mesh to prevent the parents from eating the eggs or the newly hatched fry.

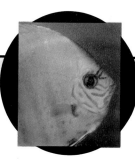

The two small photos on this page are life-sized photos of week old discus fry which are eating from the rim of a plate. The rim has been smeared with a powdered egg preparation which is Jack Wattley's secret formula. It is probably simply powdered egg available as a baking product. He gives all of the details in his book.

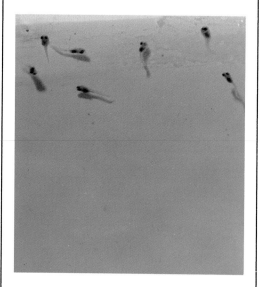

freely; they starved because they wouldn't accept any powdered egg. Jack Wattley later told me about successful results of artificially raising discus and brought me some of them. Microscopic examination didn't reveal any pathogens.

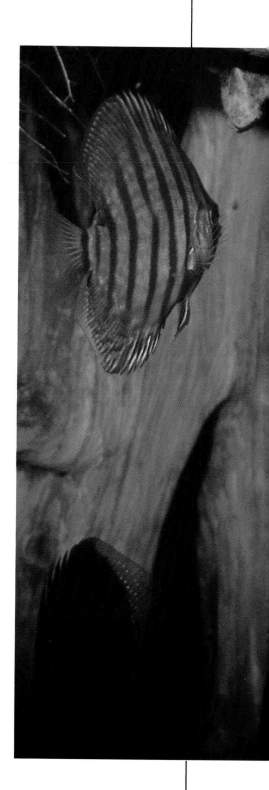

The centerfold is a photo of a very pretty crossing between a green and blue discus.

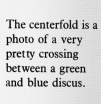

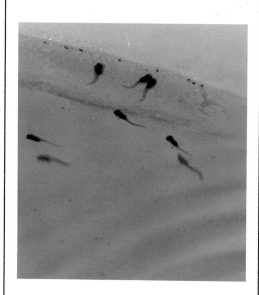

DR. EDUARD SCHMIDT-FOCKE

57

CLEARCUT ADVANTAGES OF ARTIFICIALLY RAISING DISCUS

When discus are raised without their parents the young remain healthy because their parents don't transmit any diseases to them. The important thing is that the clutch, along with the spawning pot, be transferred to clean water with the same pH and conductivity as that in the breeding tank. To make doubly sure not to transfer disease, the clutch can be transferred first to an intermediate tank containing some acriflavine or methylene blue as a disinfectant.

With good aeration, the eggs develop within twenty-four hours, and in another thirty-six hours the fry swim free. These young are then transferred to flat dishes the inside of which have been previously coated with powdered egg paste (made with water). Jack Wattley developed his method of artificially raising fish after years of experimentation. He wanted to explain it all to me, but I turned him down because I know how trying and laborious it is for a professional breeder to depend upon someone else's methods. So I sought my own way to find success in artificially breeding discus.

The larvae didn't accept powdered egg mixed with various dry feeds. It

Wattley removes the eggs from the breeders. He uses hollow white plastic piping about 5 inches tall. The eggs shown here are green because they have been developing in a fairly strong solution of methylene blue. The heavy dosage doesn't seem to affect the eggs. The lower photo shows the small, all-glass, one gallon tanks in which Wattley hatches his discus eggs.

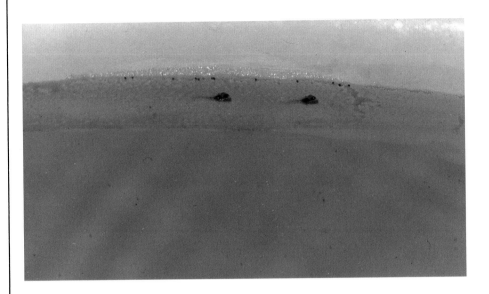

Nine day old discus feeding on Wattley's powdered egg which has been smeared around the inside edge of a plate.

wasn't until I read an article by Dr. Heinz Bremer and Dr. Ulrich Walter from East Germany that I discovered what mistakes I had made. Studies of the skin of pairs with young show, simply stated, that for the first few days the young live from a secretion of the distal skin cells mixed with epidermal cells.

Histochemical studies showed that the skin secretion contains only carbohydrates and fats in low concentration. The fry also pick up bacteria along with the secretion. These bacteria contribute to the intestinal flora. Without these bacteria, the fish won't be able to digest protein later on. The pancreas is not yet mature enough to produce digestive juices. The average aquarist is faced with almost impossible problems when it comes to artificially raising discus. We can hardly explain how Madson nevertheless

managed to artificially raise discus. Perhaps his powdered egg had already been colonized by bacteria from the tank, which the young fish then ate with the powdered egg.

The hormone prolactin can elicit the skin secretion in discus (Blum, 1974). Carefully made skin smears can provide the secretion to mix with powdered egg and then feed to the young. This is, however, an arduous method, and can, moreover, transmit ectoparasites such as *Dactylogyrus*.

My best results were with the American powdered egg that Wattley brought to me. The quality of the powdered egg is very important. Powdered egg issued to American soldiers is the best. The German product, presumably stored for a long while, proved unsuitable.

Errors in the initial feed

Jack Wattley flanked by two of his metallic turquoise discus. Wattley and the author are goood friends and cooperate in all their discus research.

composition cause most of the deaths among the young. Survivors are miserable, oval-shaped specimens. I mixed the powdered egg Wattley brought me with royal jelly and flower pollen. Indians have reportedly survived famine by eating flower pollen. According to Professor Joirisch from the USSR, pollen contains carbohydrates, vitamins, enzymes, and hormones. Young fish fed on Wattley's mixture don't seem to be any different from young fish left with their parents. Those

artificially raised young discus showed, when they grew into adults, no change in brood instinct, since this is inherited.

Water in the breeding dishes soon became turbid because of the egg powder. So I bored a hole through the center of the dish and inserted a plastic tube stuffed with a lady's stocking; with a thin tube from the prepared water in the tank above it, like a medical infusion or drip, water was led into the plastic tube at a controlled rate. The overflow flowed through

the stocking filter.

Constant transfers, as I did in the beginning, caused fin and abrasion damage to the young fish. All of these methods take time, effort, and money, but result in quickly growing young fish free of parasites.

The simplest method is to remove the young of a well-caring pair on the fifth to sixth day and raise them separately, if they're ready to feed on *Artemia*. If you wait longer, they can be attacked by ectoparasites. This is how you obtain healthy discus stocks with which further good breeding can proceed. The prerequisite is treatment of the parents to control the almost always present gill worms and other worms.

Considering the bad experiences with medications which have discouraged me, I give only short baths. What worked well was a bath with 15 grams salt per liter or one with 5 cc of formalin concentrate to 100 liters water. The fry shouldn't be transferred before being given formalin baths, for netting them could injure their skin and let formalin enter through the wounds. Short baths lasting from ten to twenty minutes should be given only while the fish are being watched carefully, as already mentioned. These baths don't affect any *Capillaria* nematodes in the gut.

Based upon reported

successes and the alleged harmlessness of Flubenol in the control of gill worms, I place my pairs in a Flubenol bath for a day before they spawn. I've not had any bad results.

The essential point is that the young *Artemia*-fed discus be removed from the parents as soon as possible to avoid their picking up *Capillaria* eggs from the bottom or their being infested with gill worms. Even longer formalin baths can't completely destroy gill and skin worms.

Before catching the young fish with a soft net, thoroughly vacuum up the bottom of the breeding tank and replenish with water of the same pH and conductivity. The young are transferred from the moist net to prepared

The Klaus Eckert cobalt blue discus with the green tinge.

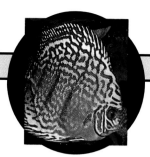

water containing trypaflavin. This water will be replaced. Despite this procedure, I never lost any young fish, though they had faulty stripes, even when they were transferred to old water.

In an effort to discover any errors I might have made, I gave some of these fish to experienced breeders for their comments. Except for the stripe and gill defects, all comments were positive. Health, appetite, and good growth were verified. These were from red discus captured near Alencer.

It would be interesting to see whether the red coloration will again occur once the diet is changed. It's probable that this method will allow raising healthy offspring from wild parents and that the next generation of young can also be raised apart from their parents without any problem.

These fry are a cross between a brown discus, *Symphysodon aequifasciata axelrodi* and a hybrid discus shown partially in the background. It is much easier to cross tank-raised discus than wild discus.

Discus Varieties

SYMPHYSODON AEQUIFASCIATA HARALDI FROM RIO PURUS

Prof. Dr. Herbert R. Axelrod discovered the green-blue discus in the Rio Purus in Brazil. At the same time he found the cardinal tetra there in the town of Tapaua. This photo is the actual fish he found.

In 1960 I succeeded in breeding green-striped discus from fish collected for me in various

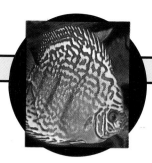

Beautiful turquoise fish about 6 months old. This was derived from the Rio Purus discus which are now supplied by Adolfo Schwartz.

localities by Harald Schultz. Then I received a visit from Willi Schwartz, the late owner of the Rio Negro Aquarium in Manaus, Brazil. Mr. Schwartz was a congenial Austrian who emigrated to Brazil, and was known as the discoverer of the armored catfish (*Corydoras*) species named after him. Millions of neons and also *Symphysodon discus* Heckel were shipped mainly to the U.S.A. and to Europe from his extensive holding facilities in Manaus. He also kindly cooperated with scientists such as Professor Geisler,

who has been my friend for forty years. Schwartz took these scientists along to his collection sites. Professor Geisler gave him information on the discus habitat, especially the water characteristics, which are so important to aquarists.

Discus don't live in the black water of the Rio Negro, which is too acidic and poor in food organisms. They live instead in a confluence of black, white, and clear waters, mainly in the tributaries on the left side of the river.

The water composition of the Rio Negro varies

seasonally; values recorded by Geisler are:

Total hardness: 0.0-0.27°DH; Total nitrogen: 280-390 micrograms; Conductivity: 7.7-22.8 microSiemens; pH: 4.2-6.2

The lower water values in the Rio Negro area were possibly also the reason why the breeding of Heckel discus at first caused me greater problems than did discus captured elsewhere.

The habitat of *S. aequifasciata haraldi* and *S. aequifasciata axelrodi* is found in the tributaries of the Rio Purus, which, in turn, is a southerly tributary of the Amazon.

Here are the water values for the Rio Purus: Conductivity: 128 microSiemens; pH: 6.6; Total hardness: 0.6°DH; Iron: 1.3 milligrams (conspicuously high).

These values interested me particularly because discus from the Rio Purus are more red-brown in body color. There are still no studies as to whether iron in feed animals or iron in the water is assimilated to give that color to the discus. It is, however, probable that the redness is from the carotene content of the food animals on which the fish prey. Geisler found

The so-called German red turquoise.

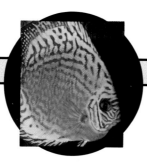

These are the result of inbreeding and selecting the Purus discus. Note the high form of these fish and the deep blue cobalt.

freshwater shrimp up to 15 cm (about 6 inches) in size. All captured discus were the same size. So adequate food must be available. Wild discus which have suffered periods of starvation have faded colors.

What is important for us aquarists is Geisler's finding that discus don't need water of a constant composition and that a change in water chemistry during the rainy season could stimulate reproduction.

My own observations show that readiness to spawn is greater during low atmospheric pressure and rainy days than during periods of high atmospheric pressure.

Discus live in the tributaries of the Rio Purus in mixed, turbid water among twigs and uprooted trees. Visual depth is only to 1.0 to 1.2 meters. Water temperature ranges from 28 to 29°C (about 82 to 84°F). All this means for discus enthusiasts is that bright illumination over the breeding tank makes the fish nervous. It disturbs breeding and brooding and incites the fish to eat their eggs. None of my breeding aquaria are illuminated.

The first discus I received from Schwartz were a colorful mixture of brown, partially and completely longitudinally striped fish. The conclusions: *Symphysodon aequifasciata axelrodi* and *S. a. haraldi* occur together

in the same waters. Willi Schwartz gave the name *royal blue* to bluish striped discus. It was conceivable that the blue stripes were caused by more black pigment cells, in contrast to the turquoise green from the same biotope. The most beautifully shaped discus came to me from the Rio Purus region. The males were particularly characterized by a high dorsal fin. These variants can be obtained by selection and inbreeding. The ancestors of the high, solid green discus likewise came from the tributaries of the Rio Purus.

THE GREEN DISCUS
In 1960 Dr. Axelrod invited me to give a talk in Chicago on my experiments with *Betta splendens*. Almost at the same time, wholesalers returned from a collecting expedition bringing green discus allegedly from the Leticia region. That was the first time green discus—there were supposed to have been about 90 of them—were captured in such large quantities.

These new arrivals were at first called Discus Tarzoo, and then later assigned to *Symphysodon aequifasciata aequifasciata*. Dr. Axelrod brought me to the owner of the Rainbow Aquarium,

The light cobalt blues are also derived from the *Symphysodon aequifasciata haraldi* from the Rio Purus in Brazil.

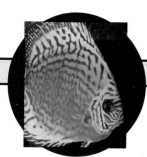

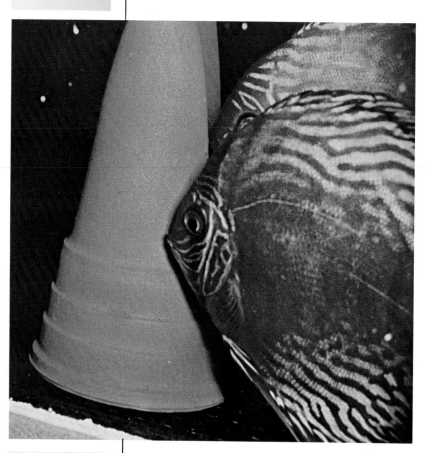

These two photos are the early proofs that the author provided to show that he had spawned the wild *Symphysodon aequifasciata haraldi*, the blue discus.

Harald Schultz collected and photographed this fish at Lago Téfé, in Brazil. It is the very rare *Symphysodon aequifasciata aequifasciata*.

Mr. Kyle Swegles, in Chicago, whose father was killed on this expedition.

Along with journalists and many onlookers, I admired two green discus males in full color and threat postures just opposite me in an exhibition tank. By skillful dealing, Dr. Axelrod acquired both of these priceless fish and gave them to me. I also received from another dealer two damaged green females marked with pea-sized red-brown dots on their flanks, unlike the males. En route to Frankfurt, my plastic bags leaked, and a friendly stewardess helped me to seal them. With little water and wet trousers, I finally got the wild specimens alive to Frankfurt.

Despite optimal care, the females took over a year to recover. After that, one pair produced a large brood. A few I gave to the aquarium at the Frankfurt Zoo, where they lived quite well for five years.

Intestinal and other worm infestations didn't occur with the first wild specimens. Since that time, mainly green discus from various localities, especially Lake Téfé, have been imported. Most show only little color. Gray-green on the flanks, pale

The author's study of the wild *Symphysodon aequifasciata haraldi*, the blue discus, with its offspring. This photo, a part of the series, was the first truly documented spawning of this species.

green stripes on the head, and only rarely some decorative brown-red dots. The characteristic, though, is the rich black band through the head, back, and caudal fin.

Heiko Bleher supplied me with selected discus of all species and subspecies which he brought back from his collecting expeditions. I received a pair from the Téfé region that far surpassed the first green ones in magnificent color. Males and females were sprinkled with brown spots on a brilliant green body ground color.

The breeding of this pair I left in the hands of several experienced breeders in order to disseminate the unusual coloration. Photos sent to me later of these fish showed that breeders who

After Harald Schultz died, I asked Prof. Dr. Herbert R. Axelrod to investigate the area around Téfé and see if he could find any more of the discus that Harald Schultz had previous found. Axelrod went there in 1974 and found two different color varieties, the green shown above and the blue. Both are *Symphysodon aequifasciata aequifasciata*. These fish probably were the basis of the so-called German red turquoise.

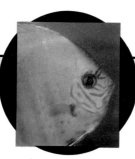

Crossing the two subspecies of *Symphysodon*, namely, *S. a. aequifasciata*, the green discus, and *S. a. haraldi*, the blue discus, results in colorful discus like this one.

had adequate natural feed available obtained young discus with the same coloration as the parents. My own, however, fed on a monotonous winter diet, looked dull and homely— an indication that pigment must be supplied through the diet if the natural coloration of discus is to be brought out again. Moreover, I received wild specimens from Rio Putomayo which were almost completely striped in green and hence could be called *Symphysodon aequifasciata haraldi*. These fish, however, likewise exhibited the typical black band on the fins and also a slight red stippling. I can't say whether or not they are a natural cross of *S. a. haraldi* and green discus. Flooding during the rainy season could mix discus into other river systems. Harald Schultz reported that among numerous blue discus *(S. a. haraldi)* in a community, he found two specimens sprinkled with pea-sized, blood-red spots. That shows how difficult it must be for ichthyologists to distinguish the individual subspecies of discus.

Prof. Dr. Herbert R. Axelrod collected this magnificent specimen which he preserved and submitted to Dr. Leonard P. Schultz at the Smithsonian Institution requesting that it be named to honor Harald Schultz. Thus this is the type of *Symphysodon aequifasciata haraldi*, photographed while it was alive.

Green discus,
*Symphysodon
aequifasciata
aequifasciata*, from
the Rio Putomayo.

The author's portrait of the first *Symphysodon aequifasciata haraldi* imported alive into Germany.

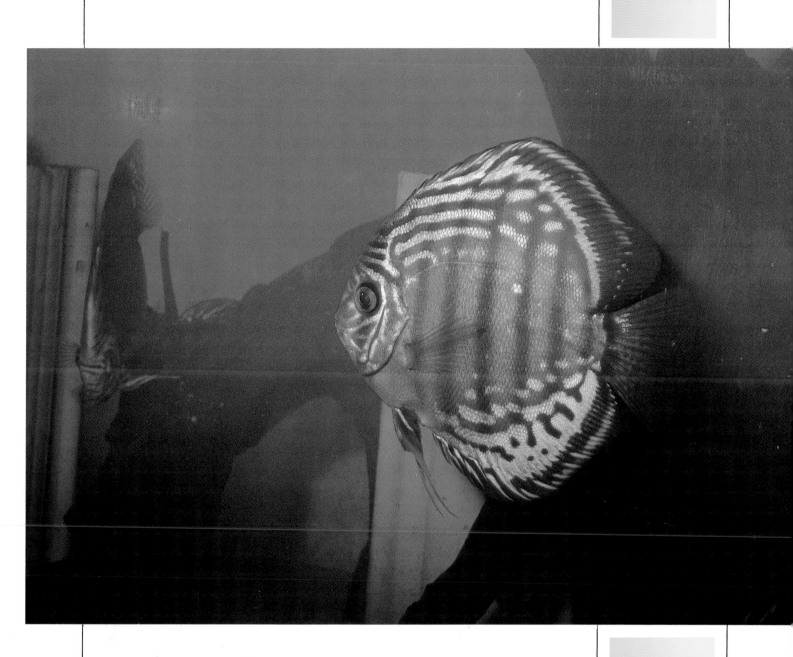

An enhancement of the coloration in a green discus from the area around Téfé. Discus from this area differ because some are found in the lake and some in the river.

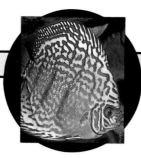

To the right is a *Symphysodon discus discus* crossing. It has the objectionable black stripes. No one has yet bred the other discus subspecies, *Symphysodon discus willischwartzi*, the pineapple discus from the Rio Abacaxis that Prof. Dr. Axelrod discovered.

The fish below is a red male of the Alencer strain.

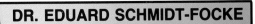

The red spots are a characteristic of many wild cichlids, not only discus. The intense red spots are found on some Téfé discus, while the paler spots are Rio Putomayo fish.

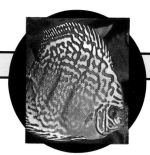

RED DISCUS

More than ten years ago I obtained the first genuine wild red discus specimen, a female in excellent condition and carefully isolated from the other fish. According to information received, it was caught in the Rio Icana. Red discus are among the rarest of color variants. A broad black band on the dorsal, caudal and anal fins is typical of all red discus. This band also passes through the anterior part of the fish and is delimited by a narrow green fringe on the fins toward the body. Individuals also show a deep black fifth diagonal, similar to that of the Heckel discus. This diagonal is probably not sex-specific.

I can't say whether these red color variants are related to the brown discus (*Symphysodon aequifasciata axelrodi*) or to the green discus (*Symphysodon aequifasciata aequifasciata*), which likewise has a black band on the fins. I purposely didn't undertake any laborious scale counts.

What I call the red discus, others call the brown discus. This is the red discus, *Symphysodon aequifasciata axelrodi*.

Here is a female red discus, *Symphysodon aequifasciata axelrodi*, from the Rio Icana.

Such a count would necessitate sacrificing a specimen or anesthetizing it for quite a while, with consequent damage to the skin.

The intense red coloration of the Rio Icana discus is caused by red cells. It's probably a reflection color which appears fully only in direct light and changes according to refraction. Fright can turn the Rio Icana discus pale. Flank color can then become brown or yellowish. The red coloration is most intense in sunlight or under proper fluorescent illumination.

The photographer Hans Mayland took the best pictures of my first red discus, which he often published in his books. I myself haven't had any success in the many attempts I made to take pictures which would have clearly shown the red color of these fish.

To maintain the red color, I paired a red female with a turquoise green-striped male who had a brown ground color. This was *Symphysodon aequifasciata haraldi*. I

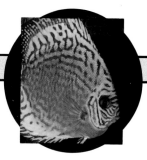

This is the real brown discus, *Symphysodon aequifasciata axelrodi*. It is the topotype that Prof. Dr. Axelrod photographed before he preserved it. It comes from the lower Amazon near Belem do Para. Note the black ring across the base of the dorsal, caudal peduncle and anal.

tried to breed a turquoise-striped discus with red ground color by inbreeding and selection. The first inbred generations were stippled turquoise or weakly turquoise-striped, with brown-red ground color. Only in the fifth generation were there sporadic appearances of light green-striped specimens with red ground color.

There were fewer and fewer black pigment cells (melanophores) as this selective breeding proceeded. The actual number of melanophores becomes apparent once such a discus becomes sick, at which time these black pigment cells are scattered netlike over the whole fish. Sick discus usually are dark-colored and stay in a corner of the tank. Half-black discus have nerve damage.

A. Pieter made good photos of the cross-bred fish. I found that their brilliant, contrasting colors made them the most beautiful discus I've ever seen. Hobbyists call this color variety red turquoise. Every discus enthusiast, however, has his own ideal standard of beauty.

I've always stayed away from crossing discus from different localities, and I've tried to maintain the characteristic colorations of each geographical race. I was therefore quite excited in the fall of 1987 when I received red discus from a river near Alencer.

These discus have the typical black band on the fin fringes. In the spring of 1988 I received four red discus, two of which showed the prominent fifth diagonal. I noted numerous lesions, and holes left by lesions, on the heads of all four specimens. I had already noticed the same thing in a shipment of over a hundred green discus from the Téfé region. These lesions responded to treatment and healed up after treatment with metronidazole and an increase in temperature

to 35°C (95°F). The fish continued to grow and are in the best of shape, though two clutches weren't fertilized. Other attempts to breed them will be made.

Is the fact that both of these clutches laid by wild specimens were not fertilized any evidence that medication can make discus infertile? Or could the increased temperature have been the cause? In mammals, the testes are outside the body, and heat treatment of the testicles in mammals has caused sterility. Considerations of this nature lead us to avoid any more heat treatment of discus.

We can never be certain whether the coloration of wild red discus specimens is caused exclusively by red pigment cells or by pigments assimilated from the diet. I again obtained a hereditary red ground color after cross-breeding and inbreeding.

Jack Wattley's friend, Colonel Fernando de Lacerda, reported that he had caught red discus. After these red discus had been held several weeks at the collecting station, they lost their redness.

The Indians in this region of jungle paint themselves conspicuously with red vegetable pigments that protect them from insect bites. Fernando, and also Harald Schultz earlier,

found out that this color is obtained from tree bark. Insect larvae assimilate this red pigment. If these larvae are eaten by discus, there will most certainly be a transfer of pigment to the fish. Red discus, without this diet, return once again to being ordinary brown discus.

My wild specimens, however, still have their red ground color. I feed them preferably red water fleas, fly larvae (maggots), *Enchytraeus* (whiteworms), and small crustaceans that I breed myself.

Asia still supplies colored fish. Bernd Degen reports intensive red discus in Taiwan, where these discus are fed

I've tried to stay away from crossing discus from different localities because the results are so unpredictable and unstable, like the fish shown here.

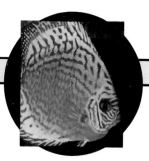

This is not a healthy discus. The black may very well be a melanoma, similar to that found on swordtails. There are, however, half-black varieties of angelfish, but they have never become popular.

freshwater shrimp. These shrimp provide the discus with large quantities of carotinoids. It's still unclear whether the iron content of the water plays any great role in the red coloration of fish.

I once received some very emaciated, sick blue discus, *Symphysodon aequifasciata haraldi.* The head area was sunken in, the ground color dark brown, the eye color black. The normally brilliant blue-green stripes were scarcely visible. These fish had a long period of starvation behind them, so I have to assume that expression of the natural colors is dependent upon diet. After two months of varied diet, however, the fish again exhibited brilliant colors. This is evidence for association between food supply and color. Coloration is naturally also affected by mood and fish "psychology."

RED DISCUS DISCOVERED AT ALENCER

Heiko Bleher caught three red discus females in a river near the city of Alencer. These red discus were not different externally from Rio Icana red discus, although the Alencer region discus didn't have any intensified fifth stripes, like some Rio Icana fish. The Alencer females showed a pronounced red-brown ground color. The males were more brown-red, with pale green longitudinal striping on the flanks! The intense black band on the fins, too, was present. It ran toward the body, bordered by a narrow green stripe. Is this coloration sex-specific? Breeding of the wild specimens in captivity will provide some answers. The specimens I've received up to now don't yet permit any definite answers.

I received these red discus immediately after they were collected. They didn't show any injuries and were in good shape, and they were the liveliest discus I've ever kept. The first pair spawned in only a few weeks, producing 236 fry, which the parents cared for quite well and always defended. Even as the young were being removed, the parents remained, ready to fight, at the glass wall of the tank.

These vigorous discus reminded me of the first green discus I received

Pure magnificence! This fish may be called the red pearl discus. The photographer, Fred Rosenzweig, claimed it originated from Schmidt-Focke discus. He calls it the checkerboard strain.

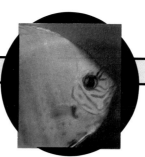

from Dr. Axelrod during my stay in Chicago. Those green specimens, too, I received immediately after collection. The males were likewise virtually uninjured.

When you consider that discus collected in the wild are usually held several weeks under unfavorable conditions at the trading post, it becomes clear that freshly collected, healthy fish can adapt more easily to captivity; they also will develop their breeding and brooding drive more rapidly.

The different coloration of the sexes in the Alencer fish doesn't imply that the females were more intensively red because of their diet. Discus fed

crustaceans and other foods that contain high levels of carotinoids develop greater expression of any red pigment cells present. The Alencer males and females had the same food, yet only the females were intensely red-brown.

HIGHLY BRED DISCUS WITH SOLID GREEN BODY COLOR

This variant is a bred form developed by several German aquarists. Heiko Bleher, of the Rio Aquarium, imported green-striped discus *(Symphysodon aequifasciata haraldi)* with intensely green longitudinal stripes from the Rio Purus region; the commercial name is

This 18-month old male is a cross between two inbred strains, namely the Wattley turquoise and my German red turquoise. My son Nils took this photo.

In 1977 Mr. A. L. Pieter took this photo of my German red turquoise.

turquoise discus. Fish like this are found in the tributaries of the Rio Purus and in the Rio Manacapuru.

The progeny from a wild pair collected in the Rio Purus and bred by a friend, Jesiorsy, in Frankfurt, included about 10% almost solid green specimens with very little expression of the longitudinal stripes.

Along with other aquarists, including Klaus Eckert and the Reverends Neff and Schulten, I obtained several specimens of these new color variants. We bred all of them successfully. The soft, weakly acidic water of the Odenwald Highlands played an important role in that success. These fish were in no way comparable with the highly developed forms that discus enthusiasts seek so ardently these days. They had pale green backgrounds interrupted by longitudinal stripes. Several hereditary factors had to be selected for and inbred to produce an intensely green body color. Progeny of these discus were the preferred variety and were spread throughout the world.

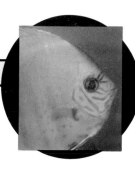

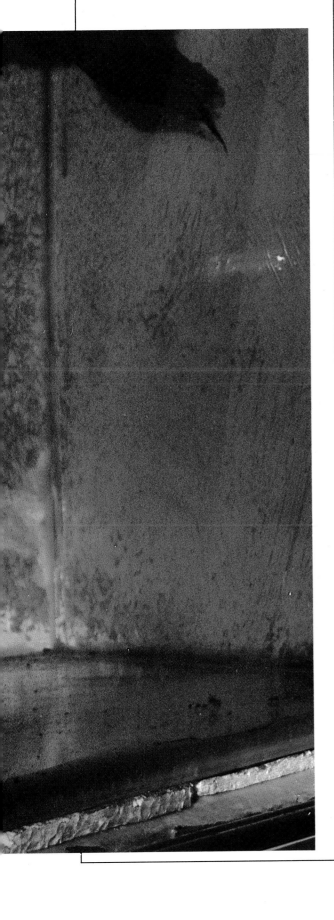

Crosses

Crossings among the discus subspecies have resulted in fish with various hues—and very imaginative names. Crosses with green discus *(Symphysodon aequifasciata aequifasciata)*, for example, have led to cobalt blue discus. The increase in the black cells of the green discus are responsible for this color. Pigment cells give discus a range of color from light green to cobalt blue. High-fin specimens, which are quite impressive fish, I obtained by selection.

The following disadvantages should be kept in mind: Ever since solid green discus achieved their great desirability, hybrids are about the only ones left in aquarists' holdings, and the natural colors of the discus are masked. Only a few discus enthusiasts still advocate keeping the wild lines pure. The author belongs to that group.

CROSSING SPECIES AND SUBSPECIES

Over the centuries, the various color variants arose in nature by adaptation and mutation. We should conserve the natural colorations and forms.

I've experimented with crosses to learn whether

One of the inbred discus from the Téfé discus. Strains like this appear readily and are very strong. Some are green and some, like this one, are blue.

Hong Kong-bred turquoise discus showing the elongated rays of the dorsal fin.

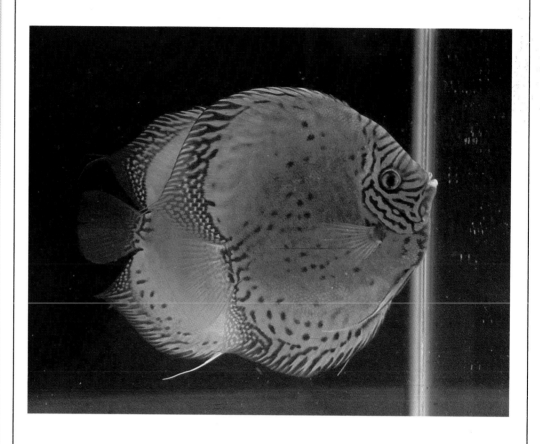

A beautifully colored female resulting from the crossing of *S. discus* with *S. a. haraldi*.

the ichthyologists' classification of discus into two species and various subspecies—*Symphysodon discus* and *Symphysodon aequifasciata,*—holds true even with crossing.

I already had experience with interspecific crossings from working with the short-finned *Betta imbellis,* which I collected on Phuket Island (Thailand) with *Betta splendens.* Both had been declared to be separate species. The progeny of the first generation (F_1) were long-

A young Japanese-bred fancy discus.

A colorful, but poor quality cross from *discus* × *haraldi*.

finned; in the second inbred generation (F_2) they followed Mendelian inheritance as short-finned (25%) and long-finned (75%). The long-finned ones, unexpectedly, were dominant over the natural short-finned form. A large number of the young were conspicuously small and weak; they finally died. The progeny of further inbred generations likewise included disease-susceptible fish. The well-known breeder E. Roloff

Two young Japanese discus derived from my stocks of many years ago.

as well as the University of Hamburg both carried out the same interspecific crosses, all with the same results.

CROSSING HECKEL × *HARALDI*

In order to determine whether discus species and subspecies can produce progeny if mated, I crossed a Heckel male (*S. discus*) with a *S. a. haraldi* female. I was particularly interested in inheritance of the fifth Heckel diagonal stripe.

The first generation was vigorous and grew rapidly. In 30% of their progeny, the fifth stripe was weak. These fish, mated among themselves, still produced progeny here and there with the dark middle stripe. One specimen had it doubly expressed on only one flank.

In over a hundred young of the F_3 generation, though, I couldn't find any with a dark middle stripe. Apparently, inheritance of the black diagonal depends upon random

Wouldn't this fish be magnificent if it didn't have the black bars? These heavy black bars are characteristic of the wild *S. d. discus* first described by Heckel. This fish came from a Heckel and *haraldi* cross.

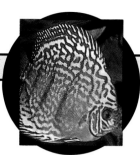

Hans Mayland made this lovely photo of a full blue discus I bred many years ago (1975).

interaction of several hereditary factors.

Jack Wattley (USA) and Lo Wing Yat (Hong Kong) attained similar results, as they informed me. They found that only 5% of the F_1 generation had a middle stripe. The experiments of three breeders showed independently that crossing species and subspecies didn't affect fertility, nor did any signs of degeneration appear. All of these experimental results raise the question of whether all discus varieties known to date belong to only one species.

CROSSES BETWEEN *SYMPHYSODON AEQUIFASCIATA HARALDI* AND *SYMPHYSODON AEQUIFASCIATA AXELRODI*

I obtained the first generation (F_1) of green-blue stippled discus from crossing striped blue discus with brown discus. Aquarists called these fish *pearl discus*.

In the second generation (F_2), the colors of the grandparents reappeared sporadically. Most of the young, however, showed an irregular pattern of stripes. In some, the color pattern was "marbled." The pattern was very attractive when red discus without green stripes were crossed with striped discus, creating "pearl discus," with their

brilliant green stippling on red ground color. Neither of these, however, are very rational crosses, because this coloration can be achieved only by crossing, and the color pattern is not consistently inherited. In my opinion, there's no fixed hereditary stock of "pearl discus" that can be obtained. It's more rational to maintain the wild forms of the discus and breed them purely with their own type.

CROSSING *SYMPHYSODON AEQUIFASCIATA HARALDI* AND GREEN DISCUS *SYMPHYSODON AEQUIFASCIATA AEQUIFASCIATA*

It's certainly an exciting experiment to cross these two magnificent fish. The blue discus came from the Rio Purus, and the green discus came from the

Even though this pair has been inbred for five generations, the heavy center bar of the fish still shows.

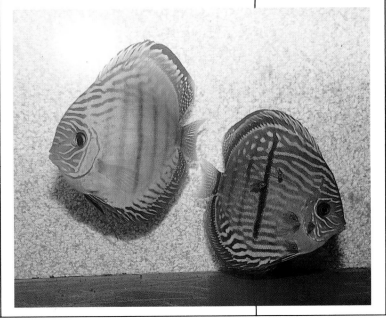

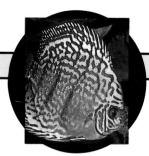

The Degen green discus, *Symphysodon aequifasciata aequifasciata*, from which I bred many offspring.

region around Lake Téfé. In the progeny of the first generation of both of these species, the black band was expressed more weakly in the dorsal fins. The red-brown stippling, too, which is typical for the Téfé discus, was only weakly apparent. None of the crosses developed the magnificent coloration of the parents. The black band on the dorsal fin is a dominant trait in green discus.

Dick Schlingmann from Dortmund in West Germany made the progeny of discus from Rio Zaraiba available to me; he had obtained them from Bernd Degen. From

photographs of his first collections from the wild, I realized that we were probably dealing with a natural cross of green and striped discus. His third inbred generation, improved by selection, showed a brilliant green, partially interrupted striped pattern on a red-brown background. There was only a hint of the black band on the dorsal fin. In contrast to my own crosses, the color here was very attractive.

In my opinion, natural crosses no doubt occur among the various discus populations after flooding of the terrain between the rivers in South America.

In my own experiments I've always been able to determine that it's possible for all discus varieties to mate among themselves. Females ready to spawn have laid eggs with males of other colorations. If mates of the same subspecies were also present, however, they were preferred. Dr. Axelrod, who participated in many collecting expeditions, found only discus of one species at a given collecting site. He never found several discus colorations together. Crosses do occur, however, in an aquarium. Discus fanciers are happy when they can demonstrate their success at breeding. Selection of breeding stock should be done only within one species or subspecies.

This is my so-called German red pearl.

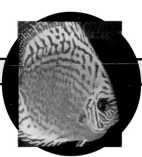

This is an inbred strain of turquoise perfected by Jack Wattley.

DR. EDUARD SCHMIDT-FOCKE

Inbreeding and Line Breeding

Decades ago I made the first inbreeding experiments with Siamese fighting fish, *Betta*

This is a 1980 strain which appeared on the Japanese market and which may have come from my stocks.

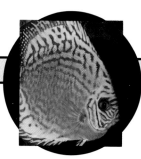

This lovely fish was bred in Japan in the early 1980s.

splendens. Of four different color strains, three degenerated after only six to eight generations of inbreeding. One group lost the fighting instinct, reacting only to partners of the same sex and never fighting seriously. In another inbred strain, pigment-cell carcinoma, a guanophoroma, appeared, diagnosed by Professor Breider of the University of Wuerzburg. This form of carcinoma could be transmitted only to fish of the same inbred strain. Bettas from unrelated strains apparently developed resistance and rejected the tumor. In another inbred strain, the ovaries of the females were formed on one side only. The fourth strain proved to be stable for inbreeding, and I bred it successfully for over seventy generations. They had no defects caused by inbreeding.

Inbreeding like that with discus is much more arduous. It takes at least one to one and a half years for discus to be bred. Harmful effects from inbreeding discus are overestimated by aquarists. Runtiness in discus is not always caused by inbreeding. Small discus, in fact, are usually a result of disease, which leaves them stunted

Cobalt blue with very high body shape characteristic of Singapore-bred fish.

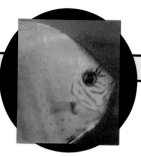

in growth.

It's possible to inbreed discus for three or four generations to fix a given color or other trait. That doesn't hurt them at all. Discus in one of my inbred lines no longer attained full growth after six generations. At eighteen months of age, these discus attained only 12 cm (about 4¾ inches) length after eleven generations of inbreeding. The clutches of these inbred discus amounted to only seventy to eighty eggs. The fertility of the males didn't abate, for they fertilized the eggs perfectly. Inbred discus are subject to the same laws that I was able to determine from preliminary studies with Siamese fighting fish, in which the signs of degeneration can be quite varied.

WHAT REALLY HAPPENS IN INBREEDING?

Chromosomes carry genetic information in opposite, duplicate genes lined up on a pair of rod-like structures. When selective breeding is practiced, especially to obtain a certain coloration, many equivalent or identical genes are accumulated, always opposite their duplicates, and this eliminates a natural state of tension that normally fosters growth. To avoid this degenerative

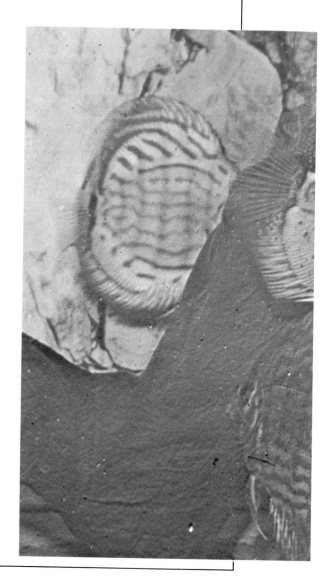

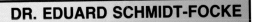 

condition, it's better to breed the same strain separated into two lines. If unfavorable effects appear in one line, then the more satisfactory fish from both lines are mated together. A selected female from line one is mated with a nice-looking male from line two, thus joining the desired traits of both fish, and also of both lines, together. This kind of breeding promises the best results in breeding discus. In all of this, don't overlook problems of timing and of place. Fast-growing discus come from healthy, unrelated discus of the same subspecies. The following chapter contains one of the secrets of successful discus breeding.

Many breeders allow their discus to pair off naturally. This is very commendable, but not very good for the development of inbred variations. Inbreeding is a technique based upon scientific facts.

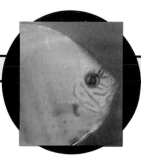

Two young
turquoise discus
from Japan.

Breeding Wild Discus

A cross between a blue and green discus in which the characteristic red spots have been selected as the prime characteristic for which to breed.

The results of breeding discus captured in the wild are very variable. Fish captured in the wild almost always have to undergo a rather long period of starvation. The

time from collection site to wholesaler in Brazil runs several weeks, during which time the fish are not fed; the only thing done for them is that the water is changed. This starvation period lasts two to three weeks, often much longer.

Wholesalers in South America keep hundreds of the captured discus in cement tanks. Food is inadequate, and usually consists of dry feed or pellets, which the fish aren't used to and don't readily accept. Feeding with live food is difficult and inadequate. Parasite-infested fish transmit these parasites and diseases to healthy tankmates. Tubercular conditions can spread more easily among weakened discus than among healthy ones.

Over one hundred imported green discus received by a dealer didn't include even a single healthy discus. Every fish in the shipment exhibited holes left by lesions (or the lesions themselves) on the head, their coloration was pale, and they were emaciated. These fish were apparently collected in one area, then kept together and shipped as one batch. Severe *Hexamita* infestation was present.

During starvation periods, the sexual organs of man and other animals atrophy because they are not absolutely necessary for survival. Life-maintaining systems are favored. In Nazi concentration camps, for example, the female inmates did not ovulate,

This was my first pair of the so-called 'royal blue' strain.

DR. EDUARD SCHMIDT-FOCKE

nor did their menses occur. I don't have any definite information, however, about sterility in malnourished males.

Among discus, mainly the males are affected; they often become sterile or at least less fertile. The females, on the other hand, generally recover more rapidly. I've mixed in "fertility vitamin" E with the feed for injured fish, but I couldn't determine whether they improved. Injection of gonadotropin would be more promising. This hormone, extracted from fish pituitary glands, is produced in Sweden, among other places.

The pituitary glands used for this purpose usually come from carp. The carp is first killed, and its head is then bored into and the gland removed. The pure hormone is extracted in a complicated dehydration process. These gonadotropin hormones retain their efficacy for years. The substance is dissolved and the solution injected into the discus, thus considerably increasing readiness to spawn.

This hormonal therapy plays a significant role, especially in fish farming. Bernd Degen plans to eventually publish a report on the effect of pituitary extract on discus fish.

Not infrequently, I

Green and brown discus were kept together when they were very young. They were fed the same food and stayed in the same tank. The brown became stronger, healthier and more dominant even though they were only 3 days older than the green discus.

107

found very well colored discus that exhibited bite wounds inflicted by predatory fish. Mr. Bleher explained to me that he learned during his collection trips how the discus with very intense coloration were the hardest to catch. He considered them to be the most "intelligent" discus in the group. I can't share that view. I believe the most conspicuous fish are seen and attacked first by their enemies. Perhaps these negative experiences forced them to develop a faster flight reaction than that of their better camouflaged companions in the group.

How long will it be before the clearing of land by fire, road building, and the mass capture of fish all reduce the fish stocks radically enough to threaten them with extinction? Mr. S. S. Rai from Malaysia wants to establish, with governmental approval, breeding facilities for captured wild discus in untouched areas of the country. First, they are supposed to be protected by nets. It's feared, however, that the Malaysian natives catch and eat discus.

SEXING DISCUS

Recognition of the sex of fish from the wild is very difficult. I received wild fish captured at various collection sites. They were selected from hundreds for good coloration.

Almost all were males. In general, *S. a. haraldi* males differ from their females in having a more intense stripe pattern. In green discus *(S. aequifasciata aequifasciata)* males, the brown-red stippling is almost always more intensely expressed than in the females. Male fish have larger dorsal, ventral, and anal fins.

Once wild fish get accustomed to captivity, they can be tested by putting a female that is ready to spawn together with what is believed to be a male. Their "bowing" behavior identifies them as a pair.

Sexing is easier in lines of the same species that have been bred for several generations. The males and females develop characteristic patterns; the males also grow faster and are therefore larger, assuming, of course, that they are not parasitized. Intestinal worms, especially, can considerably impede growth. In my solid green line the males are larger, have a higher dorsal fin, and develop their coloration earlier.

The differences are clearly defined between the sexes of discus collected from the same river near Alencer. Of six discus, all the males had a striped pattern on the flanks, while the females had a red-brown ground color and only slight striping on the head and anal fin.

In November, 1988 Prof. Dr. Herbert R. Axelrod was still at it. In the Rio Jau, off the Rio Negro, he discovered yet another color variety of discus, the bluehead. These were collected along with young aruana and brought to Manaus, then Miami, by Adolfo Schwartz. The photos show Schwartz and Capt. Raimundo Pimental, their boat and the area in the Rio Jau. This is the dry season. Normally, the discus hide in the brush during the spawning season when the river is 20 feet higher.

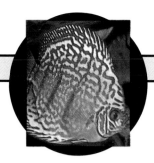

A *haraldi* and a
discus Heckel,
eating white
worms which is
my staple diet.

Discus Diet

DIET IN THE WILD

Professor Geisler found hardly any evidence of food animals in his

Bernd Degen and Dr. Schmidt-Focke. The Doctor is holding a painting showing his discus, with his face and Wattley's faded into the background.

examination of the stomach and intestinal contents of newly collected discus because their being caught makes

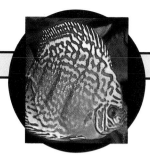

The result of a crossing between a green and blue discus.

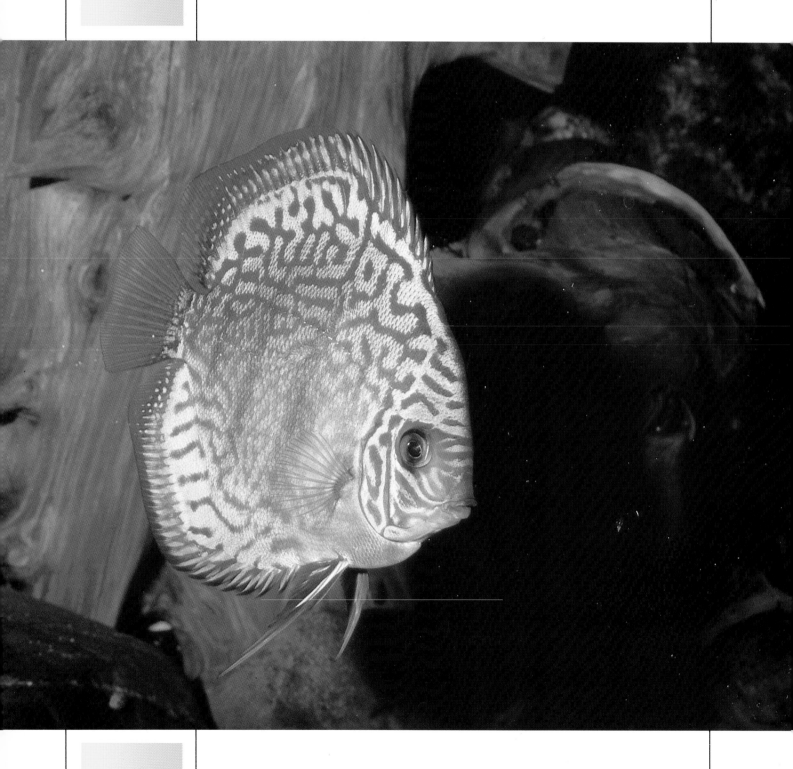

them regurgitate. He assumed that they feed on mayfly larvae (Ephemerida) and freshwater shrimp *(Macrobrachium)* found at the collection site, usually under leaves. Moreover, he also assumes that a significant part of their diet consists of algae and plants—a fact only little heeded by the discus aquarist—that provide vitamins and pigments.

For decoration of the discus tank, I use a pot of *Hygrophila polysperma.* Discus regularly eat the young leaves. So I think it's important to mix hormone-free beefheart with vegetable matter.

Organically grown spinach and lettuce leaves are particularly recommended. Rinse them off first and dry them in the freezer. Then lightly squeeze the leaves.

Bananas, carrot juice, and powdered algae are likewise suitable. The mixture will hold together with beefheart by adding the white or red gelatine used to make puddings. Discus preferentially accept red food.

I sent Lo Wing Yat young discus bred from a particularly intensely colored green pair of *Symphysodon aequifasciata aequifasciata,* and he fed them a mixture of lobster roe, shrimp, and bloodworms *(Chironomus* sp.). These fish acquired color more rapidly and better than did mine from the same brood.

Red discus I once received from Singapore lost their red color in eight weeks. They were really brown discus that presumably had been fed roe of marine animals or

These are also the result of crossing the green (*S. a. aequifasciata*) with the blue discus (*S. a. haraldi*).

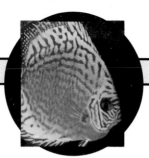

This is one of my German red turquoise with elongated dorsal rays. I fed it with beef heart which, I believe, contained growth hormones for the cow. The fish developed, but the colors were not very intense.

given red pigments. Red pigments in the diet intensify natural redness.

It cannot be our intent to simulate coloration that discus on a very varied diet don't naturally possess. Loss of color is clearly in evidence with monotonous feeding and after long periods of starvation. If our feed contains natural pigments, such as are found chiefly in crustaceans, then there's no objection to using them. Enchytraeid worms fed mainly with carrots take on a reddish color. The natural color of discus can change when pigments are supplied in the diet; some pigments or dyes are toxic and harm our fish.

GROWING YOUR OWN LIVE FOODS

What's left of safe foods for discus? One way out I see is the often laborious breeding of food animals. Years ago, Juergen Grobe brought a small amphipod, *Hyalella azteca*, into Germany from Mexico. It attains a length of 8 mm (about a third of an inch) and is grayish green in color. I let it reproduce in tanks with plants, mostly water ferns. It eats, besides water fern and algae, tomato skins and, best of all, kiwi fruit, which are first scooped out. It multiplies so well that I always have enough live food in winter. Jack Wattley brought me the similar crustaceans—but

of a yellowish color—from Florida, these yellowish scuds are seen and eaten faster by the fish. (In the first generation after crossing both species, the gray-green color masks the yellow, which reappears in the second generation.)

To make myself independent of environmentally poisoned food, I set up (despite my family's protest) twelve large plastic containers in my garden. These containers are closed to prevent algal growth. Native floating plants *(Elodea densa)* and *Ceratophyllum* filter the incident light and improve water quality. When first setting plants into the tank, take care not to also introduce snails, planarians, or leeches. I use these tanks, especially

Petshops have books on live foods. *Tropical Fish Hobbyist* magazine contains advertisements for live food cultures.

Healthy discus are always searching for food. When they stop feeding, you should start worrying.

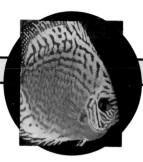

Rich Annunziata's photos of young Schmidt-Focke discus.

in summer, to breed water fleas, tubifex, and mosquito larvae.

Mosquito larvae are the best food for stimulating adult discus to spawn. Dr. Ulrich Baensch found an amino acid in them that he couldn't find in any other live food; presumably it stimulates the formation of sexual hormones.

A tubificid worm variety I discovered in a forest pond grows to a length of 8 cm (3¼ inches) and feeds on banana peels that I hang up in a perforated container.

Isopods multiply best with consistent food. Young ones, especially, are well liked. Their high chitin content promotes good digestion.

BEEFHEART

I first learned about convenient feeding with grated beefheart in 1960 from a dealer in Chicago I met through Dr. Axelrod. I brought this simple feeding method home with me to Germany. In the U.S.A., meanwhile, the use of hormones came into larger-scale use than with us. To name only a few of the hormones used, we have tried testosterone, cypionate, estradiol, and dienestrol.

During recent years, my discus males exhibited elongated, pointed dorsal fins following feeding with beefheart. Without at first recognizing the connection, I found this change in form very attractive. Hormones are

stored mainly in fat and also in muscle tissue. Reduced fertility, male sterility, and poor production of the skin secretion were apparent after long-term feeding with hormones. The average number of young was forty to sixty. I normally had 100 to 250 young from healthy parents. Jack Wattley sent young discus of one brood to two different aquarists. With one aquarist the fish developed well on a very varied diet. With the other, a busy physician, the fish received only beefheart. These fish developed veil fins, which I saw from photographs. These discus must have become sterile.

In controlled studies I learned that males of the various discus subspecies don't all respond to beefheart and hormones by lengthening of their dorsal fins. The most pronounced response was in males from the Rio Purus (*Symphysodon aequifasciata haraldi*). Controls from the same brood that were not fed with beefheart didn't show any changes in their fins.

Beefheart didn't cause any fin change in green discus from the Rio Téfé area. Reduced fertility occurred in all males fed beefheart and hormones. They didn't fertilize the eggs and ate them up. It's possible that the response

Discus kept in semi-darkness feel more at home and their colors become enhanced. The metallic blue-greens are especially attractive.

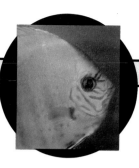

The metallic sheen developed by Wattley has been adapted by Singapore discus breeders and incorporated with the high fins. The beautiful red eye is a desired characteristic. Singapore breeders have the advantage of being able to feed their discus with unpolluted live foods.

of discus to various hormones can vary.

Discus that are fed hormones suppress their own hormone production. I still can't determine whether or not the discus males regain their fertility when beefheart and hormones are no longer fed to them. Among all the wild fish I've ever seen, I never saw a fish with elongated dorsal or caudal fins. So it's certain that these phenomena are the effects of dietary hormones.

I learned from newspaper reports that sick cows were being treated with drugs containing large amounts of hormones, so we can't really be certain that beefheart is hormone-free. That's why I've recently stopped feeding beefheart altogether and replaced it with Icelandic deep sea crab meat, crab roe, and isopods from lakes. To that I add organically grown vegetable matter. A few drops of a multivitamin preparation are added to vegetable and animal food, which is then ground up in a food processer. Agar binds it all together. Dissolve the agar in boiling water and stir it in with the feed mixture. To avoid destroying critical nutrients by this heating of the mixture, it's better to obtain from the pharmacy cold binders containing cellulose.

WHITEWORMS

Breeding enchytraeid worms—whiteworms—one of the most important food animals, gets harder all the time. Cultures I obtained from dealers were not capable of reproducing. They had been kept, presumably, in contaminated soil. These cultures consisted almost exclusively of adult worms; there were no young worms among them. Another batch contained innumerable mites of different kinds that largely devoured the feed (oat flakes for dogs mixed with vegetables). Alois Hutzinger of Austria brought me the best whiteworms. His trade secret: Bavarian dumplings as worm feed!

Whiteworms can be harvested by placing them on a warm base—a hotplate. The worms crawl to the surface and can easily be taken off. If you rinse them several times in cold water, most of the mites float to the surface of the water and can then

A discus family eating white worms which have fallen to the bottom. The lack of gravel on the bottom helps the fish find the worms.

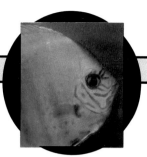

be poured off. These mite-free worms can then be used to seed a new batch.

Wooden boxes and clay bowls make good breeding containers. Spread hay and pine or fir cones on the floor beneath the boxes or bowls to improve ventilation. The soil mixture consists of de-acidified peat, sand, and forest soil. The latter has to be heated to 50°C (122°F) to keep any new parasites from tagging along. Enchytraeid worms need a temperature of 15°C (59°F). In warm countries, culturing them is very difficult. Jack Wattley, down in Florida, keeps them in a refrigerator.

A black fly about 3 mm (⅛ inch) long is more unpleasant than mites. These flies come out mainly during the summer in Europe and lay their eggs in the whiteworm containers. Large numbers of small maggots hatch and begin to eat all the food out from under the worms. The only prevention is to cover the containers with fine-mesh nylon netting. An insecticide (Psy 9) controls their reproduction. Professor Sterba was successful with moth balls. I'm not sure, however, whether or not the worms take up the toxin and pass it on to the discus.

GRINDAL WORMS (ENCHYTRAEAUS BUCHHOLZI)

Grindal worms are an easily bred food. A batch of them is placed on a moist 2-cm-thick foam mat and covered by a plastic bowl or container whose lid is perforated for ventilation. Sprinkle the foam daily with grated oat flakes, then moisten the flakes slightly with a laundry sprinkler (the kind used for ironing). The Grindal worms multiply in a short time. Then cover the foam with a perforated sheet of plastic wrap and sprinkle oat flakes over the wrap. The Grindal worms will crawl through the perforations to feed on the plastic sheet, from where they can easily be rinsed off into a container of water. Pour off the water and feed the clean little worms to your discus.

Squeeze out the foam lightly twice a week, then re-moisten it and sprinkle with oats. If you don't clean the foam, the metabolic wastes of the worms form a foul-smelling brownish liquid.

Not all foams are suitable. Some—particularly colored ones—contain toxins that can kill the worms. These worms need a temperature of 20 to 25°C (68 to 77°F). I use only undyed foam and soak it

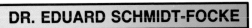

A magnificent German red high fin discus.

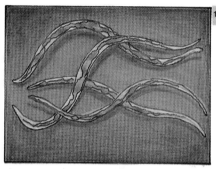

John Quinn's drawings of a typical Grindal worm culture. The worms are shown, greatly enlarged, in the top photo. A mash is made of grated oat flakes or other oat cereals. The mash is innoculated with white worms and later some is transferred to a plastic dish with a cover, from which the worms are retrieved for feeding the fish.

in water for a long time.

Grindal worms can also be cultured on peat that is soaked in water and then well squeezed out. The peat has to be renewed eventually when odors caused by the worms' droppings develop.

Grindal worms are roundworms or nematodes related to the whiteworms but much easier to grow. Even adult discus eat them.

Diseases and Medications

TOXIC FEED

Increased environmental toxicity is creating more and more problems for discus aquarists in both Europe and America. Here are some examples:

A dealer feeds his discus exclusively with frozen red gnat or midge larvae *(Chironomus plumosus)*. These gnat/midge larvae are chiefly collected on a large scale in the

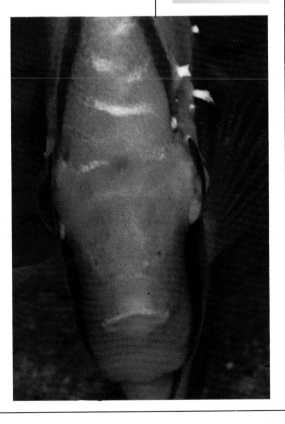

A head-on view of a *Hexamita* infection in a discus. These infections lead to 'hole in the head' disease.

floodlands of the Netherlands and also in East Asia, then shipped deep-frozen. Like tubifex worms, they live in mud and take up toxins from it, though they themselves seem to be resistant to these poisons. Feeding these organisms regularly to discus leads to chronic poisoning of the discus.

Lo Wing Yat reported from Hong Kong on damage caused by these red insect larvae. He assumes that chickens are being fattened on hormones in China and that the chicken droppings are tossed into ponds in which large numbers of larvae are cultured; they will then be shipped worldwide as cheap feed.

For experimental purposes, I obtained discus fed exclusively on poisoned red larvae. At first they refused further food. After starving a few days, though, they began hesitatingly to feed on whiteworms. I used various species of *Betta* as controls. Three pairs were selected for breeding. None of the pairs produced live young. The eggs were unfertilized. The *Betta* males seemed to be sterile. Fish from the same brood—but not fed on the larvae—produced healthy offspring. It might be advisable to first soak deep-frozen red larvae in fresh milk in the hope that antigens in the milk may bind some of the toxin.

Some years ago, I

regularly fed my discus with live water fleas (*Daphnia*) and mosquito larvae from a forest pond close to a road. As automobile traffic sharply increased, this pond presumably went toxic from rain and heavy metals. Food animals became rarer, and my discus darkened after eating the food from that site.

In another pond farther away, I collected water fleas, mosquito and glassfly larvae, and mayflies in the spring. This pond was not far from a garbage disposal site. When it rained, a trickle of turbid run-off water flowed into the pond, eventually killing all the food animals in it.

In a forest pond fed only by rainwater, I once found, years ago, a sufficient number of *Daphnia magna*. In June, 1989, I still caught water fleas in the same pond, but they are so tiny that they weren't suitable at all for my larger discus.

The pH of the pond water was 5.0. Even the acid rain contained environmental toxins. The presence of *Daphnia magna* seemed to me to be a biological proof that the pond water is still relatively non-toxic. I'm not sure, however, whether *Daphnia parva* survived. Other discus aquarists have told me they can find live foods only at great distances from the larger cities.

In my home city of Bad Homburg, near the industrial city of Frankfurt (on the Main River), there is no more unobjectionable live food. Rain water has a pH of 4.5 and an average conductivity of 40 microSiemens. These values fall even more when it rains continuously.

Municipal waterworks cannot make any definite statements on pesticides in our tap water. Analyses are too expensive and can indicate only a small portion of the toxicity.

Nitrate levels are rising everywhere. Agricultural chemicals (herbicides, pesticides) and their metabolites appear more and more in the ground water, hence also in our tap water. Sewage conduits are only partially sealed safely. When discus die, we can no longer determine whether we poisoned them with water, food, or medications. Politicians are supposed to assign urgent priority to this problem and then come up with and implement countermeasures.

HARM CAUSED BY MEDICATIONS

Once we've made it clear how clean the water is in the Amazonian home waters of the discus and how free of environmental toxins that water is, it's easy to understand that all drugs must be harmful to discus. Crystals of

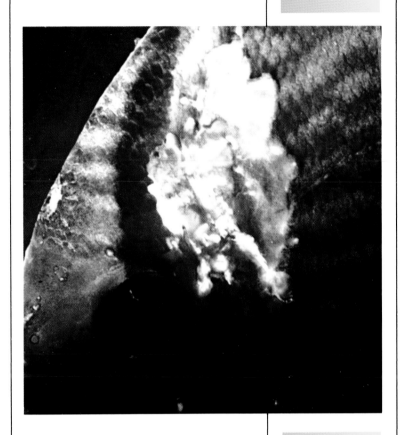

This Heckel discus is severely wounded by *Hexamita* infection.

medication have been found in the gills of discus. Nor are kidneys and liver spared damage by drugs.

Remember how many human drugs had to be withdrawn because of noxious side effects? Drug therapy for even more sensitive fish, too, can be dangerous. Therapeutic drugs used for ponds and fish farms are hardly suitable for discus. Mr. Bleher made available to me for study five young discus from each of five different breeders. I didn't know who these breeders were.

In one brood I couldn't find any parasites, aside from various flagellates and ciliates. The discus were about 8 cm (3⅛

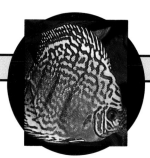

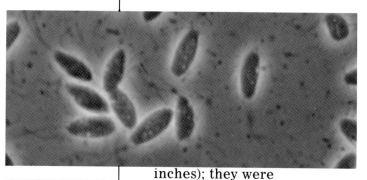

This is what *Hexamita* looks like under a microscope.

When you bring in new fish, like the one on the facing page, you should de-parasitize it as much as possible. This fish temporarily lost its color (the black bars are missing) due to the prophylactic treatment against parasitic worms.

inches); they were emaciated and wouldn't accept any food. According to Bleher, these fish had been treated with drugs about ten times for various diseases. The gills were pale, the intestines empty, with the liver gray-yellow and reduced in size. Even the parasites had left their moribund hosts. The other four broods were without exception affected by gill and skin worms. I found *Capillaria* and *Hexamita* in the intestines of most of the discus. In specimens from another brood, I immediately spotted a worm-like parasite, even at low magnifications, because of its snake-like movements. It was a *Philometra* species.

Intestinal worms can easily break through a previously damaged or weakened intestinal wall and from there infest other organs. The entry of bacteria into the abdominal cavity then leads to peritoneal ascites. The swimbladder is compressed by the fluid that develops. The fish swim around, head down, with a bloated abdomen. None of the therapeutic measures I took had any apparent success.

EXPERIENCE WITH CONCURAT (BROAD-SPECTRUM ANTHELMINTHIC)

Intestinal worms are among the most dangerous of the organisms that can affect discus. Midge larvae killed in a Concurat solution and fed several times to the fish didn't effect any permanent cure.

Further trials with an injection of 4 grams of Concurat dissolved in a liter of water, then administered via a thin plastic tube directly into the esophagus, were astonishingly well tolerated. Slight pressure on the gills makes the discus open its mouth wide. Slowly inject 2 to 3 cc of the solution. If you merely injected it into the mouth, most of the medication will run out through the gills. Afterwards, to prevent re-infection, the fish should be transferred to a prepared tank. After treatment, no more living worms will be found in fresh droppings, although the worms' eggs—apparently undamaged by Concurat—do indeed appear. Upon autopsy, I found capillarian eggs not only in the female worms but also in various intestinal sections of the discus. The Concurat injection was repeated weekly. My concern about organ damage led me to discontinue this treatment method, too. The important thing is to keep things clean in and

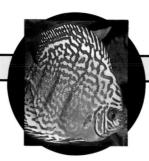

Discus and most other fishes are very sensitive to poisoned water, especially heavy metal. Regular water changes are very necessary for keeping discus in good health.

around the aquarium, and that goes a long way in preventing disease.

I don't want to go into detail on the methods for treating common discus diseases, because I consider them outmoded now. Therapeutic recommendations can be found in the ordinary literature on the subject.

When treating with antibiotics, keep in mind that useful bacteria are killed along with the pathogenic ones. This applies also to bacteria in biological filters. Diseases are frequently transmitted when aquarists trade their breeding results around. (Quarantine is a good way to control this problem.) Every tank should have its own net and its own siphoning hose. Central filters carry a great risk which is not essentially lessened even by using ultraviolet lamps.

DISCUS DEATHS CAUSED BY TOXINS IN WATER

In 1985 I learned for the first time that captive discus had started to die in great numbers. This occurred almost simultaneously on various continents; the deaths were attributed to a new, unknown pathogen.

I began wondering when I heard from other aquarists that the disease often occurred following only a slight water change involving the addition of tap water. The discus at first darkened, and then their respiration

increased and heavy mucus formed. Then the fish died. This disease has never yet stricken my fish, so I can only pass on the information I have received from others.

I live in the north of Bad Homburg. The tap water there is mountain water with a conductance of 150 microSiemens and a pH of 8.0. The southern part of the city receives a mixture of river and mountain water. One of my discus friends there lost almost all his fish, affected by the symptoms described above.

In Austria, a discus breeder inadvertently bought sick angelfish which were captured in the wild. He used the same thermometer for the angelfish tank and for his healthy discus without first disinfecting the instrument. All died from the same disease within a short time.

Along with a discus friend, Emran Pishvai, from Oregon, I visited a wholesaler who kept his fish in tap water only. All the discus were darkened in color and covered with mucus; they all "staggered" about. Other cichlids, especially the angelfish, were breathing belaboredly at the surface. I presume that this disease begins with the noxious substances in the tap water. Discus react allergically to these substances by increased production of skin secretion—an ideal culture medium for the

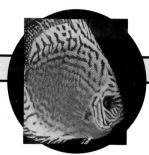

Toxicity of several metals to fishes

Element	TL_m* (mg/L)**	Probable Safe Concentration (mg/L)**	Extenuations
Aluminum	0.3 (24 hr)	≤ 0.1	Maximum solubility 0.05 mg/L: at pH 7, at least 5 mg/L at pH 9
Antimony	12 to 20 (96 hr)	—	Antimony potassium tartrate toxicity to fathead minnow
Arsenic as arsenite	1.1 to 2.2 (48 hr) 14.1 to 14.4 (29 da)	≤ 0.7 —	May be concentrated in aquatic food chain as an additional source under natural conditions
Cadmium	0.01 to 10.0	≤ 0.001	Related to water hardness, environmental factors, fish species and others
Chromium	5.0 to 118.0 (96 hr)	≤ 0.05	Related to water quality; depends on valence (hexavalent or trivalent chromium) and chemical species
Copper	3.0 to 7.0 (48 hr)	≤ 0.015	Related to water hardness, synergisms and antagonisms of other substances in the water and fish species
Iron	0.1 to 10.0 (24 to 48 hr)	≤ 0.03	Solubility of iron is related to pH; iron hydroxides precipitate onto gills and suffocate fishes at pH 7 or higer; toxicity is related to hardness
Lead	1.0 to 7.0 in soft water, 400+ in hard water (96 hr)	≤ 0.03	Solubility of lead related to pH; toxicity related to water hardness
Manganese	2.2 to 4.1 (24 hr)	—	Permanganates are much more toxic than other manganese species; manganese compounds are unstable and precipitate as manganese oxides or hydroxides at pH above 7.5
Mercury	1.0	average total mercury 0.0005	Biological accumulation 0.5 mcg Hg per g of wet weight aquatic organism
Nickel	5 to 43 (96 hr)	≤ 0.03	Toxicity is related to water hardness
Silver as sulfide + thiosulfate complex	0.004 to 0.2 280 to 360 (96 hr)	0.0001 to 0.0005 16 to 35	Toxicity is related to organic loading of the water, silver, species and other factors
Uranium	2.8 to 135.0 (96 hr)	—	Toxicity is related to water hardness
Zinc	0.87 to 33.0 (96 hr)	≤ 0.05	Toxicity is related to water hardness and to synergism or antagonism of other substances in the water

*TL_m is the "median tolerance limit," where 50% of individuals survive a specified toxicant level for a specified time period.

**mg/L is equivalent to mg/kg, since one liter of water weighs one kilogram.

parasites present in every tank. Malignant variants of various organisms arise and can also affect healthy discus.

My own experience is not sufficient for me to make any definite therapeutic recommendations. It seems to me important, however, to detoxify the tank water with activated charcoal and peat and to raise the temperature to 32°C (89°F). After a day, remove the charcoal and peat and then aerate vigorously. Subsequent administration of tetracyclines and sulfonamides has led to cures.

In summary, the new discus disease is primarily caused by noxious substances in the water, leading to excessive secretion of the mucous or slime glands, and hence to an enormous increase in parasites.

HARM CAUSED BY X-RAYS

During my medical training, women believed to be having twins or an extrauterine pregnancy were subjected to several X-ray examinations. Radiation dosage was higher then than in subsequent years. I was concerned because embryonic cells are particularly sensitive to ionizing radiation, so I studied X-ray radiation on a stable line of *Betta splendens* inbred for more than seventy generations.

The bettas' progeny were almost the same in color and shape as the parents, thus making any mutations easy to spot. The irradiation was done with the help of Dr. Kruse in a Hamburg gynecological clinic. The bettas received a dose of 10 to 10,000 Roentgens. Bettas that received 3,000 to 10,000 units became sterile. The progeny of fish irradiated with weaker doses exhibited serious physical damage. The belly was swollen, much as in ascites. Even fish (0.5 to 1% of them) that received only 10 Roentgens showed the same symptoms.

I had hoped in vain for positive mutations. In the progeny of those dosed with 10 Roentgens was one female with eyelids on both sides which she could open and close voluntarily; this fish was, unfortunately, sterile. Fish that are shipped by air shouldn't be X-rayed.

These studies had to be discontinued because my specialist training was over and I lacked funds to continue. A Dr. Proewich in America, however, let me know he had treated angelfish and *Betta splendens* with radium, but he didn't report the exact dosage. His irradiation of the fish produced black angelfish and black bettas, of which I received a few. I wasn't able to find any external damage. The black females of both species were sterile. I

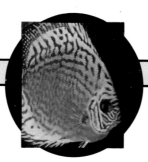

When live foods such as *Daphnia* are introduced into the discus tank, it is quite possible that you are also introducing parasites. That's why it is best to use newly hatched brine shrimp. The heavy brine prevents any worms from thriving in the hatching solution.

obtained progeny only from the irradiated black males, not the angelfish females. The F_1 were all checkered black. The F_2 generation included black, checkered, and normally colored young. I obtained gray progeny in the F_1 generation of *Betta splendens*. Mated among themselves, the F_2 split—just as with the angelfish—into black, gray, and normally colored bettas.

To my surprise, further generations of the black angelfish included sporadically appearing fertile females. I have no explanation for this result. I had no idea of the X-ray dosage given during luggage or baggage checks at the airport, and it would most likely vary from place to place. A high frequency of congenital anomalies and cancer is to be expected from the nuclear reactor accident at Chernobyl. Genetic damage like that is usually inherited recessively; that is, it is "hidden."

The Future

The Nobel Prize winner Konrad Lorenz was also a discus enthusiast, and he

Many extremely colorful discus are yet to appear on the market. While I don't like the heavy black lines of the wild discus, some people find them very attractive.

invited me to visit with him at Seewiesen. His aquarium took up almost a whole wall. In it swam healthy brown discus and angelfish as one

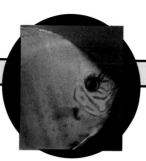

community. This tank enjoyed optimal conditions. The lighting was so installed that it dimmed gradually before darkness fell. It was fascinating to watch how the parents used the twilight: they chased after their young until the very last one had been corralled into their assembly area.

Professor Lorenz belonged to those personages who have deeply and lastingly impressed me. Up until the end of his life, he was firmly convinced that human insight would prevail, that the spirit of invention and of intelligence would eventually prevent destruction of all life. Lorenz had confidence in the younger generation's well-founded spirit of rebelliousness, and despite his severe illness he participated in their demonstrations.

For the following reasons I don't share that optimism, except with limitations:

That drive for power, aggression, and sexuality have for thousands of years determined the actions of man. This is part of the human genetic make-up and will hardly change. The many senseless wars in the past and present, corruption in most nations of the earth,

cannot—despite technical and scientific progress—positively affect human morality. Seldom have we learned from the past.

Concern with success and the thirst for profit rule public life more strongly than the rule of reason can inspire responsibility for man and environment. Visionaries and those who look ahead have up to now been unable to assert themselves in our society.

The constantly rising birth rate must be controlled. It would be difficult to effect any behavioral changes in the face of tradition and religious teachings. Considering the population explosion, there's no other way.

Professor Grzimek recognized this problem and recommended intrauterine pessaries in addition to birth control pills. A spiral inserted into the uterus prevents pregnancy for about two years. Experience from my own gynecological practice showed that in 2 to 3% of the cases the pessary was expelled. Infections, too, occurred. I vouch for this method, too, with the conditions, however, that the pessary is sterile and is placed by a trained professional.

Uprooting of trees and new housing developments are

destroying huge forest areas. Irreparable damage is being committed. Enlightenment and effective countermeasures are urgently required if the annihilation of nature reserves is to stop. Aquarist associations and ornamental fish hobbyists should stand up more for natural conservation. Discus are among the most sensitive species—and their future is utterly endangered.

Discus kept in dimly lit tanks show up better than do brightly lit fishes. The dimmer aquarium is more restful for its owner, too.

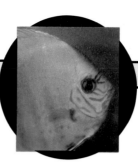

Raising fancy discus can be a profitable as well as fulfilling experience. When baby discus are feeding well, they will have droppings almost constantly visible on some of the group. No droppings means they are not feeding! Be observant.

Closing Words

Destruction of the environment brings discus aquarists a growing

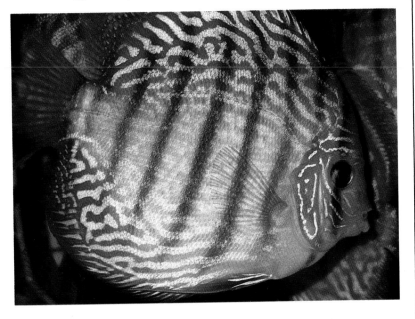

This fish is in a brightly lit aquarium and most of its colors have faded.

number of problems.
Contamination of drinking

A high fin discus obviously with lots of *axelrodi* blood in it as can be told by the black ring around the fish. The black ring starts at the base of the dorsal, runs through the caudal peduncle, onto the anal fin and then across the stomach, through the eye and back to the dorsal.

water, particularly in industrial nations, but also in East Asia, causes a lot of worries and is responsible for the mass death of discus. The nitrate levels are rising in agricultural areas. The use of pesticides and herbicides is continuing. Some of this contamination has already been detected in rainwater. Fish in the ponds near large cities are dying. Our usual wild-collected food animals for our fish are getting rarer. Water fleas in rain puddles or ponds in my vicinity no longer attain the size of *Daphnia magna*. Tubifex worms and red midge larvae contain toxins picked up from the soil.

It's advisable to grow your own live foods. Dry

Bernd Degen makes real pets out of his fish and he can hold them and feed them from his hands. My tanks are too large and too high to try such a thing. This is Degen's hand and one of his exquisite discus.

Manfred Goebel
bred this fish from
Wattley's strain
which originated
in the Rio Jurua.

DR. EDUARD SCHMIDT-FOCKE

feed, microworms, Grindal worms, and whiteworms don't suffice as a complete diet. The culture of fast-growing amphipods (scuds) in aquarium tanks has been successful. Oceanic animal foods, too, are a further possibility. Keep in mind, though, that changes in the tastes of discus as they grow older can become a problem.

Beefheart often contains, despite loud assertions to the contrary, hormones that can lower fertility and cause sterility in discus males. Another sign of hormone problems is elongated dorsal fins in males.

Environmental toxins and metal traces can be 80 to 90% removed from tap water with reverse osmosis devices. Activated charcoal and peat likewise remove contaminants, but to a lesser degree. Discus diseases have increased at an alarming rate.

Intestinal worms are the most dangerous. Almost all medications contain toxins which harm the organs of discus fish.

Healthy discus lines are obtained by artificial—though laborious—breeding. Disease transmission from parents to young can be controlled if the young are removed in time from their parents.

Discus of different origin should be kept separately to prevent any focus of infection and disease. It's advisable for each tank to have its own inlet and outflow. Not even a drop of water should go from one tank to another. Daily changes of water (⅕ to ¼ of the total quantity), using prepared water, make biological filters superfluous.

The natural coloration of wild discus should be maintained. I've only crossed discus to study the inheritance of traits and to investigate fertility.

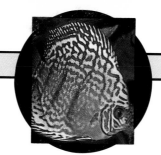

Index

DR. EDUARD SCHMIDT-FOCKE

Suggested Reading

ALL ABOUT DISCUS
By Dr. Herbert R. Axelrod;
supplements by Dr. Leonard P.
Schultz, Guenther Keller, Dr.
Gottfried Schubert, Dr. Robert J.
Goldstein, Jack Wattley and Dr.
Robert W. Burke
ISBN 0-87666-761-2
TFH PS-669
This book brings together the
experience of many of the
world's leading experts on the
subject. It is an excellent book
for everyone who keeps discus,
whether beginners or advanced,
as just about all the information
on this interesting fish species
is contained in this book.
Written on the high school
level.
*Hard cover, 5½ × 8″, 135 pages
54 black and white photos, 41
color photos.*

HANDBOOK OF DISCUS
By Jack Wattley
ISBN 0-86622-037-2
TFH H-1070
This is the standard American
classic about discus with tips
and techniques from an
acknowledged expert.
Contents: Introduction.
Background of the Discus.
Collecting. On the Classification
of Discus. Equipment. Water
Chemistry. Purchasing. Food.
Spawning. Discus Keeping
Around the World. Diseases.
The Most Famous Fish Breeder.
*Hard cover, 8½ × 11″, 112 pages
Over 100 full-color photos.*

DEGEN DISCUS
By Bernd Degen
ISBN 0-86622-086-0
TFH TS-134
For all aquarium keepers and
breeders of discus, this is an
essential book on their care.
Written by a leading discus
authority, this book reveals
inside secrets to successful
raising and breeding of discus,
and is filled with beautiful
color photos of these majestic
fish.
*Hardcover, 9½ × 12½″, 112 pages
Contains over 150 full-color
photos.*

DISCUS: How to Breed Them
By Bernd Degen
ISBN 0-86622-641-9
TS-137
Bernd Degen, internationally
recognized for both the high
quality of his discus and the
large numbers of them he's able
to breed, has provided a
revealing overview of European
approaches to breeding the
most sought-after of all
aquarium fishes. How to select
discus, how to develop a
breeding line, water chemistry
for breeding discus,
preparations for breeding,
helpful tricks and secrets—all
this and much more is covered,
complemented by over 100 full-
color photos that show the full
range of color varieties.
*Hardcover, 8½ × 11″, 128 pages
Contains over 100 full-color
photos*

**DR. AXELROD'S ATLAS OF
FRESHWATER AQUARIUM
FISHES**
By Dr. Herbert R. Axelrod and
others
ISBN 0-86622-748-2
TFH H-1077
Here is a book—a truly
beautiful and immensely
colorful book—that satisfies the
long-existing need for a
comprehensive identification
guide to aquarium fishes that
find their way onto world
markets. This book SHOWS IN
FULL COLOR not only the
popular aquarium fishes but
also the oddballs and weirdos,
not just the warmwater species
but the coldwater species as
well, not just the foreign fishes
but the domestic species too.
Information about the
essentials of each fish's
maintenance is presented with
the photos in easy-to-read
symbol form. Fully indexed by
both common and scientific
names.
*Illustrated with more than 4500
full-color photos
Hardcover, 8½ × 11″; 800 pages*

**HANDBOOK OF FISH
DISEASES**
By Dieter Untergasser
ISBN 0-86622-703-2
TFH TS-123
Handbook of Fish Diseases is by
any yardstick the finest, most
useful book about fish diseases
ever offered to aquarium
hobbyists. It is so valuably
instructive, in fact, that it will
be just as useful to owners of
pet shops and tropical fish
specialty stores and will raise
the quality of aquarium fishes
all over the world. Colorful,
comprehensive and completely
understandable, the book is
loaded with needed information
and good advice that will save
money and fishes' lives
wherever it's put to use.
Because of its simple style, this
magnificent volume makes the
diagnosis and treatment of fish
diseases easier and surer than
ever before. Keys to recognizing
fish diseases and giving the
right treatment are provided in
easy-to-follow charts
accompanied by excellent full-
color photos, all taken by the
author and never before
published in an English-
language book. By noting the
symptoms a fish shows, readers
can use the keys to isolate the
cause of the disease through the
process of elimination and
simply follow up with the right
treatment (also listed, of
course). A more foolproof
system has never been devised.
Chapters on fish anatomy, viral
and bacterial diseases, fungal
and algal diseases, parasites,
tumors, genetic abnormalities
and much more are
supplemented by sections
dealing with valuable
techniques such as staining and
microscopy. The book also
contains an extensive listing of
drugs for treating fish diseases
and, where possible, sources
from which they can be
obtained.
Contents: Recognizing Diseases.
Fish Anatomy. Viral and
Bacterial Diseases. Fungal and
Algal Diseases. Pathogenic
Protozoa. Worm Diseases.
Arthropods. Diseases Not
Caused by Specific Pathogenic
Organisms. Treatment of
Diseased Fish. Microscopy
in the Diagnosis of Fish
Diseases.

*Hardcover, 8½ × 11″, 160 pages
Over 100 full-color photos by the
author.*